MONEY FROM HOME

Where the Money Hides Behind the Screen

A technical assessment of the most viable online businesses to make money from home with the skills you already possess

© Copyright 2019 - All rights reserved.

The contents of this book may not be reproduced, duplicated or transmitted without direct written permission from the author.

Under no circumstances will any legal responsibility or blame be held against the publisher for any reparation, damages, or monetary loss due to the information herein, either directly or indirectly.

Legal Notice:

This book is copyright protected. This is only for personal use. You cannot amend, distribute, sell, use, quote or paraphrase any part of the content within this book without the consent of the author.

Disclaimer Notice:

Please note the information contained within this document is for educational and entertainment purposes only. Every attempt has been made to provide accurate, up to date and reliable information. No warranties of any kind are expressed or implied. Readers acknowledge that the author is not engaging in the rendering of legal, financial, medical or professional advice. The content of this book has been derived from various sources. Please consult a licensed professional before attempting any techniques outlined in this book.

By reading this document, the reader agrees that under no circumstances are is the author responsible for any losses, direct or indirect, which are incurred as a result of the use of information contained within this document, including, but not limited to, —errors, omissions, or inaccuracies.

RETURN POLICY

It will be my goal and the intent of this book to provide you with valuable, insightful and accurate information about Making Money from Home. I believe that if you have purchased it, it is your desire to learn about all of the risks and rewards, and possibilities of becoming an online entrepreneur and engaging in this type of venture.

However, we are all different with our own unique style of writing, presenting information and viewpoints. What I may see as important or valuable, you may not find to be so. Because your satisfaction in your search for knowledge is very important to me, I want to offer you a 7-day, no questions asked, money back guarantee on Amazon. Simply follow the instructions below to return an Amazon Kindle Book and begin your return under Manage Your Content and Devices:

- Go to www.amazon.com – your account
- Navigate to "Manage your content and devices"
- From the "your content" tab, select the Action [...] button next to the title you want to return, and then select Return for Refund.
- In the pop-up window, select Return for Refund

HOW TO GET THIS KINDLE BOOK FOR FREE

This book is enrolled in <u>Kindle Matchbook</u> so you can get it **for free** when you buy the Paperback version.

DOWNLOAD AUDIO VERSION OF THIS BOOK FOR FREE

If you choose to agree to the <u>FREE AUDIBLE TRIAL</u>, Amazon will allow you to download the audio version of this book for free. After the trial period, you will have one free credit per month to listen to any of the 200,000+ titles available on Audible, and you can cancel when you want.

BUSINESS TOOLS AND LINKS ON-THE-GO

I do hope that you will keep it though and not only enjoy the book, but use the information within to change your life and the future of your children. As you go through the book, **you will find a <u>hidden password at the end of each section</u>. You can use this password to access a handy tool in the form of a pdf file with a Quick Reference Guide to help you on your journey. The PDF summarizes the businesses assessment contained in this book, plus a list of extremely useful, online tools in a printable, <u>clickable</u>, handy, on-the-go version.**

Please download this file especially if you purchased the paperback version, so that you can easily connect to the several link, tools and resources listed in this book.

Go to EMCPress website to download it:
www.emcpress.com/

PLEASE DON'T FORGET TO LEAVE A REVIEW

Lastly, if by the conclusion of this book, you have been inspired, motivated and informed and ready to step out on your own, **my only request at that time is that you leave me a review on Amazon** for future entrepreneurs. Let me know what you liked most about it so that I can be sure to include this in my future books as well. This is vital for my work and for the work of many entrepreneurs that will likely read this book to start a profitable online business.

Thank you,

Larry B. Fossett

Table of Contents

introduction ix

Chapter 1 Are you an entrepreneur? 1

    Risk 2

    Positivity 4

    Self-motivated 6

    Passion 7

    Money 8

    Curiosity 10

    Independent 11

    Challenges 13

    Tech savvy 15

    Some people are born to it… 17

Chapter 2 Skills you Already Possess 19

    Skills 21

    Passion 25

    Problem-solver 26

Chapter 3 Online Business to Avoid 31

    Sustainability 32

    Long-term 35

    Profitable 36

    Scams 38

    Mystery Shopper 41

    Multi-Level Marketing 43

    Binary Options Trading 47

    Gambling and Betting 48

Work-from-Home 50
Chapter 4 Real and Viable Online Businesses 56
    Amazon FBA 59
    Self-Publishing on Amazon 71
    Ghostwriting 83
    E-bay and Ecommerce selling platforms 94
    Dropshipping 102
    Turnkey Websites 113
    Gaming 119
    Affiliate Marketing 125
    Online Courses 147
    Additional Options for online businesses 153
Summary 157

INTRODUCTION

If you have picked up this book, you must be interested in developing and sustaining a long-term online business. Of course, starting any business is nerve wracking and scary, especially for a new entrepreneur. The unknowns in a traditional, brick and mortar business have been tested, experienced and challenged for years and the "experts" have written the book on the how-to's, ins and outs and ways to be successful.

But the world of the Internet, a mere several decades old, brings new uncertainties, challenges and of course, opportunities. It is understandable that you may be unsure how to get started, afraid to fail and eager for help. You will find this book to be a solution to your problem!

Becoming an on-line entrepreneur is not the big boogey man in the closet or under the bed, nor is it out of reach. Through "Making Money from Home", we will walk through the process of identifying and evaluating the skills that you already possess to determine how you can best use them to start your business. We will assess the many opportunities that the Internet offers. To bring awareness to the risks and dangers that are also present, this book will address the wrong, dangerous or unsustainable businesses. Lastly, we will look at how you can use your valuable skills and qualities to begin and operate a viable and profitable online business.

Each of us probably has our own reasons for wanting to start our own business. But there are certainly many common factors that tie the community of entrepreneurs together. Owning your time, flexible hours, being your own boss and pursuing your passions are more than likely at the top of the list and in fact, just scratch the surface. As you consider this idea of creating your own business, you must keep in the front of your mind what your personal reason is for starting on this journey.

- Is it to have more time with your family?

- Are you tired of the 9 to 5 rat race, making someone else rich?

- Do you dream of the day when you can pass on a profitable business to your children and grandchildren?

- Would you like to guarantee a comfortable lifestyle for you and your family?

No matter what your personal WHY is, there are a huge number of benefits of starting your own online business.

Of course, there are the obvious ones like family time, money and the flexibility to work wherever you want. But there are so many other benefits of working from home for a business that *you* have started. Before we go on, think about how that last statement made you feel; proud, excited, accomplished, successful. If starting an online business is able to make you feel all of these things, imagine what you can do for others by starting it.

Not only does the opportunity to become an entrepreneur impact you and your family. Consider how you can impact your target audience or customers by providing them with a solution to a problem. Imagine what you could do for others as your business expands; providing job opportunities for others, helping them to create personal wealth, and enhancing your own philanthropic efforts.

Of course, there is a more tangible reality to your business venture. You have the opportunity to pursue your passions and create your own work environment; one that is conducive to you and your style of working. You get to meet new people and network with other entrepreneurs and up and coming business owners. Achieve a level of financial independence that most only dream of. Have the ability to travel and to explore new cultures. Develop a schedule that fits around your new lifestyle, working how much or how little you want, spending time with family and friends. The list goes on and on. Lastly, and maybe most importantly, leave a legacy for your grandchildren and a great story to tell.

If any of these benefits or advantages has touched a nerve or sparks an emotion within your soul, then you may be ready to move forward and have made a wise decision in reading this book and learning more about how you can Make Money from Home.

By using the skills that you already possess and the suggestions that you will see throughout this book, you can learn how to take advantage of the infinite number of opportunities that are at your disposal. You can build the life you want and have always dreamed of; you will earn the money that you need; you can create a prosperous lifestyle for you and your family.

You may be leery whether you can really be successful as an online entrepreneur. You may have heard of friends who have tried it and were not successful. They may have given it a half-hearted go at it and given up, going back to the stability of a 9 to 5 job. However, there are many others out there who have overcome the failure, fought through the challenges and dug within themselves to create a successful online business. Let's look at some of these entrepreneurs who have come before you, starting their own businesses online and creating the lives that they have dreamt of.

If you consider how the global, mammoth of an online business began, you may be amazed to find out that Jeff Bezos of Amazon started his online business as an online bookstore in 1994. While scouring the depths of the then-infant World Wide Web, he stumbled across an astounding piece of data: Internet usage was increasing by 2300% per month[i]. He just knew that he needed to jump on that train. Immediately after evaluating his own skills and researching the top items that may sell online due to size, accessibility and low cost, Amazon.com was spawned. Currently employing nearly 650,000 workers worldwide, Amazon has become the top digital company in the world as of 2018[ii].

GoDaddy.com, web domain registrar extraordinaire, was started by Bob Parsons, a retired U.S. Marine when he realized that he was not ready to retire. His unique philosophy of "making a little money from a lot of people" has proven to be wildly successful and a cornerstone for web hosting for entrepreneurs around the world.

You certainly have heard of Amazon and GoDaddy, so let's look at some smaller, lesser known, though highly successful online entrepreneurs.

By age 21, Neil Patel's name had been added to the Top 100 Bloggers list by Technorati. He was labeled a "web influencer" by the Wall Street Journal [iii] and has successfully launched several Internet companies, specializing in SEO and digital marketing. Patel has now been named one of the Top Entrepreneurs under 30. However, he started somewhere just like you. As a 15-year-old with an entrepreneurial spirit and a good work ethic, Neil began his business journey selling cable black boxes and auto parts.

Tung Tran, a 25-year old affiliate marketer, knows how difficult the world of online business can be. After failing several times and losing a significant amount of money in the process, he never gave up, constantly learning and pushing forward. Although his family and friends thought he was delusional and wasting his time, once he found his niche and began earning revenue, he knew he was onto something. He became passionate about increasing his knowledge, earning a nice income and most importantly, turning his online business into a career.

Six years later, Tung Tran has established several successful online businesses, earning him bragging rights as one of the 8 Successful Online Entrepreneurs You Should be Following by Entrepreneur.com magazine.

Then there is Jason Zook, founder of IWearYouShirt.com. After the recession in 2008, Jason decided he wanted to create an online business, wearing t-shirts for companies. During the next five years, Jason produced videos, created posts and blogs featuring and advertising the logos and catch phrases for thousands of companies, earning him a cool $1,000.000. Jason shared his story of success with CBS Evening News and Forbes Magazine[iv], describing how he came up with the idea, his process and how the company ran its course before he decided to end it. This is a perfect example of a successful company that shut down, not because of failure, but its founder moved on to other business ventures.

As you can see, opportunities are endless for entrepreneurs at any age, at any stage of life, in a limitless number of areas. In this book, it is my goal to walk with you on your journey to entrepreneurship. From the first desire to start your own business, to your self-doubt and self-analysis, to your trial and errors, I promise to guide you, provide you with support, and help to connect you with the vast digital world around you. We will discuss how you can be a solution to someone's problem, just as I will be a solution to yours.

I will teach you how to research and identify online business opportunities, niche markets and target audiences. I will share with you the many traps, scams and risks that are also associated with online businesses. I will provide you with proven techniques for reaching your audience where they are and connecting with them to persuade them to not only want your product, but to feel that they *need* your product or service. I will show you how to maneuver through the complicated, yet exciting world of online selling, dropshipping and marketing. Lastly, I will encourage you throughout the book to use your own unique skills and qualities to develop, operate and succeed at creating a life that you love and are proud of.

It is my ultimate goal to help you to experience the joy and satisfaction that you can have from not only earning a profit for your efforts but in knowing that you are creating a sustainable business that you can pass on to your family for generations to come. I want to motivate you to become part of a unique group of people worldwide who have also stepped out to create, develop, help, and inspire through their creativity, motivation and effort. What makes these entrepreneurs unique is their ability to follow their passion and their own personal why, to challenge the conventional way of doing things and then to enjoy the results of their labor.

The world behind the screen moves at a rate of speed that is faster than everyday life. New businesses spring up on the web faster than can actually be recorded. Internet opportunities come and go, morph and change, enter and exit the fast-paced digital world. Although figures vary from several different sources, it is estimated that 100 million new online businesses are created around the world each year. That is almost 274,000 per day! At the same time, 100 million businesses close. This constant fluctuation and entrance and exit of businesses provides tremendous opportunity for you, the entrepreneur. Not all businesses that start will fail, and not all those that close have failed. There are opportunities everywhere, hidden in plain sight, and with some research, ingenuity and effort you too can take advantage of these business opportunities.

What are you waiting for? Will you be one of the many to say that you always wanted to start your own business but didn't, or will you be one of the those who takes that leap and starts an online business? The decision of course is completely yours. But, understand as basketball legend Michael Jordan has famously said, "you will miss 100% of the shots that you don't take". In other words, how do you know if you will succeed or fail in your business venture if you never take a step to make it happen! I can assure you that you will not become an overnight millionaire or make the Top 100 Entrepreneurs list by sitting back and doing nothing!

We all know that fear of failure is real. It is true that businesses fail and companies go out of business. But look at the world around you! Everything in your space was inspired, designed, created and made by SOMEONE! Someone who went out on a limb, possibly risking it all, because of a desire, a passion, a thought or a feeling. You could be the next one that the papers are writing about with your new business idea, method or product. It is certainly a possibility but time is of the essence. The more that we delay, the more that we tend to convince ourselves right out of a decision. You are reading this book, so there must be a reason why you picked it up. There is something stirring in you that makes you want to be better, to live more, to earn more, to be freer. Don't hesitate, but instead pursue what it is you are after and go get it. But go after it knowing that you are not alone.

You've heard about a single event, product or message that inspires and motivates someone to change their life. Why not let today be the day and "Making Money from Home" be the catalyst to take your life to a new level, to change your income, your lifestyle and your future generations. Be true to yourself along the way and enjoy the process!

CHAPTER 1

ARE YOU AN ENTREPRENEUR?

According to the Merriam-Webster Dictionary, an entrepreneur is someone who "organizes, manages and assumes the risks of a business or enterprise".[v] This definition opens the door to so many thoughts and questions. Are people simply born to be an entrepreneur? Can you develop the skills necessary to become an entrepreneur? Do I have what it takes to go out on my own to organize, manage and assume the risk of a business?

You probably are aware of some of the big-name entrepreneurs who started their careers as college dropouts, not being able to hold down a job: Mark Zuckerberg, Bill

Gates and Steve Jobs. Aside from dropping out of college, these three men have many things in common. They possess certain skills and characteristics that separate them from the rest. Let's look at some of the qualities which may be the thread connecting these as well as many other entrepreneurs.

If you are interested in becoming an entrepreneur, let's explore what it takes to be an entrepreneur.

Risk

Many people can be responsible for organizing and managing a business. However, it is the risk that separates those who can from those who cannot. It is this inclination to take, or rather not shy away from risk, that puts the entrepreneur in a class of his or her own. Being a risk-taker is a predisposition to take advantage of an opportunity or in fact, to create their own with the expectation that it will reap some type of reward. Taking a risk of any size or magnitude requires the risk-taker to acknowledge that there is uncertainty and as much possibility for failure as there is for success.

Throughout life and even each and every day, we as humans take risks. We risk being hit by a bus while crossing the street. We risk losing our job to a younger or more experienced employee. We risk financial ruin by mismanagement of our money. However, the risks that a person with an entrepreneurial spirit is willing to accept are different.

Risk-taking and entrepreneurship go hand in hand. If you are evaluating if you have the ability to be an entrepreneur, let's first evaluate your willingness to take risk.

You have a steady paycheck while working your 9 to 5 job. Although you may be dedicated to your j.o.b., you arrive promptly at 9 and depart exactly at 5. Becoming an online entrepreneur may mean giving up the security of your current situation. As an entrepreneur, you will likely have to put in more than the standard 40 hours per week. However, the reward may be in both financial gain and accomplishment. In all likelihood, you will dedicate your life to this endeavor and may lose the ability to go back to the job or career if the venture does not work out. Are you willing to take that risk?

Right now, you can bank on next week's paycheck and probably have been for a very long time. You may be squirreling away extra cash, paying off debt and living comfortably. If you decide to leave that job and step out on your own, you may need to invest your own funds as well as you may not earn any more for a while. You may have to stretch your wallet and risk being uncomfortable financially.

It is possible that if you left your 9 to 5 and yet despite your best efforts, your business venture may not be as successful as you had hoped. You may find yourself having to start over, managing the emotions and feeling that go along with this.

There is certainly a risk of failure that is inherent in becoming an entrepreneur. You must decide if you are willing to take a leap of faith and pursue it although there are risks involved. You must be willing to make some tough decisions as well as personal and financial sacrifices along the way.

Positivity

You have to believe that there is another way of making a living than simply the daily grind of a 9 to 5. A positive attitude and belief that the future is bright and full of opportunity will be necessary to carry you through the tough times. By surrounding yourself with good, quality people, you can ensure that you have a positive environment, with supportive role models and mentors.

Those with an entrepreneurial spirit are usually optimistic and positive. They value their own time as well as that of others more than money itself. If you want to become an entrepreneur, you must ask yourself if you see positive results in the future and if you do not have the mindset, you must be willing to change to become a more positive person.

It has been proven that negativity attracts negativity and positivity attracts positivity. Through the Law of Attraction[vi], we understand that 'what you give out to the world is ultimately what will return to it'. If you walk around with a negative attitude, giving off negative energy, that same energy will come back into your life, possibly impacting it in another way.

How can you expect for your business venture to succeed if your perception of people, your life and the world is all doom and gloom! Entrepreneurs think positively and are sensitive to negativity and the impact that it can have. They believe that not only do they have the power to change their life, but of those around them as well and they strive to do so.

Self-motivated

Knowing your personal 'why' is the first place to start when considering becoming an entrepreneur. Why do you want to be an entrepreneur in the first place? What makes you get out of bed every morning? Motivation is the thing that drives you to your goal. It is the thing that fuels your ability to put one foot in front of the other. It transforms your current life into something that you have dreamt of. It is the rocket fuel behind your propulsion to accomplish huge and amazing things.

Being the type of person who takes the bull by the horns and steers life will drive you to your destination. If you simply sit back and wait for others to dictate life for you, you will be getting out of life, what you have put into it. Nothing! An entrepreneur is motivated by and driven to succeed by things he or she wants and loves. By proactively taking hold of life and seeking after the heart's desires, the entrepreneur immediately surpasses the pack and distinguishes himself from those who rely on luck for success. Successful people are successful by choice rather than by luck of the draw or by accident.

Self-motivated entrepreneurs are more willing to take risk to achieve their goals. They have a clear understanding of what they want in life and are determined to get it. They believe that the impossible is possible with dedication, positivity and old-fashioned elbow grease. Are you motivated to go after what you believe in and desire? Are you ready to take life by the horns? If so, keep reading.

Passion

Knowing your 'why' then naturally leads into determining what you are passionate about. Passion takes your motivation and your desires to the next level. If motivation is the fuel, passion is the high octane that you need in your life to succeed.

I am sure you have met someone in your lifetime who just gives you one-word answers when you ask them questions. "What are you interested in?" "Nothing." "What did you do on the weekend?" "Nothing." Then all of a sudden, you ask that one question that sparks their interest, "What did you think about that new book?" Their eyes light up, they begin to talk faster, and visibly standing more erect. That burning desire to now talk about something that interests them is the passion that each of us has for *something*. It is that thing that initiates an emotional response.

Passion can also be described as the energy or driving force to take action.[vii] Although passion alone is not going to ensure success, business without passion is also not a complete failure. According to best-selling author of *I Will Teach You to Be Rich*, Ramit Sethi, "Passion doesn't find you. You find your passion." Just because you may not be completely passionate when you begin a business venture, it does not mean that you will not become passionate.

As you develop and deepen your understanding of your personal interests in pursuit of a business opportunity, your passion will grow within you as well. This process will drive you to continue to learn, grow and become successful in whatever it is that you are working towards.

If you are not sure as of right now what it is that you are passionate about, don't worry. You'll figure it out.

Money

Of course, money is a driving force and motivator for most of what we do in our lives. However, the entrepreneur has a healthy relationship with money. If you hold onto it too tightly, you will be unwilling to risk losing it. Becoming an entrepreneur then may not be the right choice for you.

As was discussed earlier, you may have to invest some of your own money when you are first beginning any business venture. This may be difficult for someone who is extremely cautious, overly shrewd with their money or downright cheap! You may have heard the phrase 'it takes money to make money'. You cannot expect to go into any type of business without having to make some type of investment or cash outlay. There may be options available to you such as financing, grants and loans. Inevitably though, you must decide as an entrepreneur how you want to utilize and manage this money in order to invest in your future business.

Money is not evil nor is it the root of all problems. It is our perception of money and what we as consumers do with it that causes problems. Our world revolves around capitalism and everyone's ability to buy goods and services. Having a healthy relationship with money and the right mindset to manage it will give the entrepreneur the ability to properly prioritize it among life's other values.

As you consider starting out on your own, evaluate what your relationship with money is like and if you possess the right mindset to handle the risks and rewards associated with the economics of being an entrepreneur. If you don't have it now, you can certainly work on developing this quality to ensure your success as an online business entrepreneur.

Curiosity

The proverb "curiosity killed the cat, but satisfaction brought it back"[viii] is very applicable to the business world. We warn little children about the first half, telling them that they should not be nosy. But, oh the satisfaction that it brings when you are rewarded by investigating. It is part of our natural human inclination to be curious, to want to investigate, experiment and learn. But, it helps you to become an entrepreneur as well.

Entrepreneurs must always be thinking. In order to succeed, you need to be aware of the world around you, open to new suggestions and ideas and ways of doing business. Stagnation can creep in when you as the business owner are not infusing the operation with creative products, services and ways of appealing to your customers.

Curiosity opens the door to more questions and of course, more answers. In therapy, a commonly used exercise is questioning 'why'. Each time the question is asked, the answer must go deeper and is more thought provoking. By asking 'why', you may even be able to head off the possibility of failure by foreseeing a problem or challenge before it ever begins. Curiosity leads to creativity, productivity and problem-solving.

Even if you have never thought yourself to be curious about anything, think about the last time you questioned something or someone and then looked up the answer on Google. Of course, we are all curious. It all depends on what you are willing to do with the curiosity and where you will allow it to take you.

Independent

Entrepreneurship can be a lonely place. As the person responsible for the success, or failure, of your business, it is up to you to make it or break it. Unfortunately, though, the pressure and responsibility can become overwhelming, tiresome and frustrating. Many entrepreneurs experience burnout because they are too proud to ask for help.

Some entrepreneurs and business people seem to be able to do it all. They have a vision, a dream and will do anything to achieve their goals. That can-do attitude carries them far, but it also prohibits them from developing their teams and growing the business. Being goal-oriented and driven is an amazing quality, yet it can also be isolating and insular. As much as family and friends want to participate, the independent nature of an entrepreneur can at times prevent them from developing and nurturing crucial relationships in their business and personal life.

The entrepreneur takes pride in being able to take care of him or herself and their family. Because this type of person does not like to leave the warranty of the family's safety and security in someone else's hands, the idea of owning and managing a business venture is more appealing. If you are threatened by someone else having control of or limiting the amount that you can earn, you may have an entrepreneur's mindset. You take pride in the ability to earn your 'own' money to provide for your family and would you rather not have to *thank* someone for what you receive. That can-do, independent entrepreneur mentality is a quality that will serve you well as you move forward in your business venture.

Finding balance between striving to reach goals and to develop a sound business and family responsibilities can sometimes be a struggle. It can sometimes be difficult for your family or significant other to support you in this high-intensity, stressful, exhilarating new lifestyle. There will be sacrifices that may be necessary to be an entrepreneur and family person. However, if you believe that you can handle the stresses and pressures of being a business owner, keep reading.

Challenges

Losing is a part of life. So is stumbling, getting up on your feet again and trying again. Entrepreneurs believe that failure is not an option but rather an opportunity to learn. As Colin Powell said, "There are no secrets to success. It is the result of preparation, hard work, and learning from failure." [ix] Nothing is easy and there are no shortcuts.

If you have you ever heard the idiom, "if at first you don't succeed, try, try again", you will understand that failure is just a stepping stone to the next level. With each challenge, you will learn something that you can apply to either the next time you are faced with this same thing or use this knowledge for something else. With each step you rise above and move on. Just because you may have made a mistake, does not mean that you have failed. When you were learning to tie your shoes, I am sure that it took possibly hundreds of times before you got it right. Since are probably not wearing Velcro shoes today, you were able to overcome the challenge and frustration of learning and did not quit.

An entrepreneur is going to be faced with many challenges along the way. To be successful in your endeavors though, you must be competitive and willing to do anything to win. However, if you do lose, you must learn from it and keep moving. Don't let a loss keep you down or deter you from reaching your goals. A loss is simply another kind of opportunity and a means to an end.

If you truly want to be an entrepreneur, how you handle challenges, mistakes and failures will determine your success. Accept the challenge and welcome the opportunity to problem solve and to learn something. When your fight or flight response kicks in, choose to fight and keep going when the going gets tough. Of course, it will not be easy and each business venture will bring its own ups and downs, positives and negatives. It is how you handle each and every situation and what you learn from them that will determine your success as an entrepreneur.

It may be in your DNA to face challenges head on, viewing each situation as an opportunity. On the other hand, a challenge may immediately be a threat to you and your security or well-being. Either way, evaluate how you have handled difficulties in the past and what you learned from them. Whether you have cowered with your tail between your legs or you stood tall and welcomed the occasion as something to learn from, your skills will be put to the test when you take on the challenge of starting your own business working from home.

It is common for people to think that the life of an entrepreneur is rosy or that it was simple. To those people, an entrepreneur was handed a business opportunity and simply sat back and watched it grow. They do not witness the long days, and even longer nights; they are unaware of the personal and financial sacrifices that must be made; they don't see the labor before it became the fruit. But then again, not everyone is destined to be an entrepreneur. Not everyone will be able to say that they built something from the ground up and in reality, that's ok.

Tech savvy

In this extremely fast-paced, technologically driven world that we now live in, we all must be tech savvy. This is not to say that you need to be able to write code and install the latest servers. But, to begin with, you must own a computer if you want to join the community of online entrepreneurs.

All The links and tools listed in this book are available for free at www.emcpress.com in an easily clickable PDF File

If you are still using a flip phone, you may want to switch over to a Smartphone. If you are not yet familiar with the Internet, get a jump on that today.

No matter what type of business venture you would like to dive into, the savvy entrepreneur is also a tech savvy one. If you think that technology is too much for you to handle, then maybe stepping out on your own with an online business may not be the ideal option for you. We are now surrounded by and can no longer avoid the automation, telecommunication and digital technology. Making our lives easier, faster and more productive, technology has brought the business and commercial world to the next level at lightning speed. To be able to survive and compete at any level at all, the entrepreneur must know his or her way around a computer and the Internet pretty well.

Although there are many resources out there available to assist you, you as the business owner want to have a solid understanding of the tools that will support you and your business. From email communication and websites to online classes and sales opportunities, the Internet has something for everyone. As you evaluate your qualities to become an entrepreneur, be sure to consider this very important factor and be ready and willing to learn and expand your knowledge base in this area before you take any huge leap into a business venture.

Some people are born to it...

Not all of these qualities and characteristics may be innate to you. However, that does not mean that you are not destined to be an entrepreneur. Entrepreneurship is not an easy road. If you have identified with only a few of the items listed, don't worry. Some people believe that you are either born an entrepreneur or not. It is proven though that you can rewire your brain to be more positive, more efficient and more productive, each of which is beneficial to an entrepreneur. Even if you are not a born entrepreneur or never considered it before, there is nothing stopping you today from rewiring your brain, starting new habits and embarking on a new journey.

By reading this book, you will learn how to determine if you have what it takes to become an entrepreneur; to earn a long-term, passive income. You will learn how to evaluate your skills, to use what you have and to gain the knowledge to in fact achieve success.

Before we go on, if you enjoy reading this book, please take thirty seconds to **leave me a review**. Find the direct link to the Amazon Review Page on the PDF you downloaded from **www.emcpress.com**. Thank you!

Let's now look at how you can become an entrepreneur through one, if not many, online business opportunities using skills that you may already possess or developing some new ones.

First part of the password to get the PDF: lets

The PDF summarizes the business assessments contained in this book, plus a list of extremely useful, online tools in a printable, **clickable**, handy, on-the-go version. Keep reading to find the next part of the Password at the end of the next Chapter.

CHAPTER 2

SKILLS YOU ALREADY POSSESS

Now that you know what qualities and characteristics are common among entrepreneurs, and you know that you want to proceed at becoming an entrepreneur, let's look more closely at the specific skills that you possess to make it happen.

Although a degree from a college or university may have carried you thus far, it will not be as useful in beginning an online business. Of course, the skills and experiences that you acquired while studying will help you in life, managing money, business sense, etc. But in the online marketplace, no one cares what degree you hold or what your title is.

When considering what type of online business you want to start, you will need to go back to the basics. Online business is going to represent more about what you do well, rather than what you think people will want. By going back to basics, we are talking about getting to the basics of who you are and how you will be useful to consumers.

Of course, when you are considering a business, you don't simply want it to exist. The goal is for it to be successful and profitable. Why invest your time, energy, and money into something simply for it to BE! There is a process to deciding how you want to become an entrepreneur and what product or service you will offer. You don't just wake up one day and suddenly you are a successful online business person.

There are literally millions and millions of online businesses that have sprung up over the past decade, each selling, swapping, serving and offering *something*. Now consider how many more consumers of those goods and services there are. According to a study done about e-commerce, it is estimated that 1.8 billion people worldwide purchased goods online in 2018[x]. This impressive number will only grow as more and more brick and mortar stores expand their online offerings and availability and new entrepreneurs hit the scene with new and improved, faster, smarter and fancier *things*. As goods become scarcer on the shelf, there will be a greater need for goods and services to be available through the Internet.

Why not share in the proverbial pie and in interact with at least some of those 1.8 billion people! It is expected that by 2021 online sales will amount to more than $4.8 trillion globally. By developing your online business, you will not only contribute to this number, but more importantly, reap some of the benefits.

Whether you ultimately market and sell a physical good or a service, becoming an online business entrepreneur is the wave of the future. Let's get you started today.

Skills

As we look at the best and worst online businesses in the next chapters, we must always come back to the foundation of why you are reading this book and my goal as your supporter; determining what is the best online business for YOU based on your specific qualities, interests and hobbies. Of course, there are a multitude of options, choices and in fact, opportunities that you could certainly try. You could join an established team, work for a company remotely, or buy a franchise and certainly be profitable and earn a nice living.

But if you really want to do this on your own, be your own boss, then you are on the right track. By reading this book, you have already expressed that you want to experience the creative and business process from start to finish. Don't let anything hold you back or prevent you from reaching your goals. You may say that you don't have any skills or special abilities that people would want from you. You cannot be sure of that until you do a thorough evaluation of your skills and qualities. You have to really look at what you bring to the table and what makes you uniquely YOU?

You will be surprised when you begin to look at the qualities and the skills that you do possess. Everyone has something that makes them marketable to someone else. We just have to figure out what that something is. You may actually find out that you have more than one skill that will help you create your online business. It is natural for us as humans to say, "I am not good at anything" or "I don't do anything interesting". As commonplace as that may sound, it is just NOT true!

To begin exploring and understanding all about you and your skills, let's do a good old-fashioned brain dump. Write down a list of the qualities that you possess. Don't leave anything out! Don't cross off anything because you feel that it may not be relevant! If you actually enjoy washing the dishes, write it down! Leave nothing for speculation or off the table. You never know what opportunity may exist or that you may be able to develop into a business venture from one of those items on your list.

Consider these questions as you are writing and add the answers to your list:

- What do your friends compliment you on? Can you bake a mean lasagna? Are you always the best dressed in the room?

- What do people frequently ask you for help with? Are you the friend who everyone comes to for grammar and spelling help? Do you get asked to select the Anniversary gifts by all of the other husbands because your wife always loves the gifts you select?

- What do you pay other people to do *for* you? Do you want a perfectly manicured lawn? Did you purchase that beautifully arranged bouquet?

- What activities do you do in your spare time? Do you collect specific character figurines? Do you draw or paint? Do you construct historical train track replicas?

- What would you love to share with the world? What information have you studied or learned and have a large amount of knowledge about? Are you very familiar with the habits of birds?

- Lastly, what are you NOT good at? Do you detest writing? Are you horrible at spelling but want to get better? Are you a terrible driver?

Of course, this all-encompassing list will be exhausting to create yet exhilarating at the same time. You will see that the possibilities are endless. To someone looking over your shoulder, it may look like bragging rights or that you are patting yourself on the back. Absolutely not! You are getting to the root of what makes up the realm of YOU; no other individual has exactly the same skills and qualities and interests that you do.

The last items on the list, the ones that you are NOT good at, are intended to keep your mind open to possibilities. If you are not an expert at something, there is a pretty good chance that someone out there is not either. This may be an opportunity for you to improve and then teach someone else. Sounds like a business venture to me.

Passion

Although we all minimize our capabilities, we are each passionate about something. If you recall, we discussed earlier this idea of passion. Passion is that something that lights a spark within you. It motivates you to speak with people, to talk on and on for seemingly hours. It drives you to work late into the night, to break all of your personal rules and to step outside of your comfort zone.

Maybe you are that shy person, answering questions with just a one-word reply. Until that one subject comes up in conversation or the door opens for you to speak about it. Then you are gushing like a fountain to share what you know because you believe in it so passionately.

This is not to say that everything a person is passionate about can be turned into a business opportunity but you have to at least explore it. Go ahead and add that thing that you are passionate about to the list you have created and let's see where it will take you.

Problem-solver

Now that you have this amazing list, the next logical question would be, 'what in the world do I do with it?' It is proven that businesses that have the greatest probability at succeeding are those that solve a problem. Well, this throws a wrench in your entrepreneurial plans. It may seem difficult enough to come up with a market or idea, now we are talking about solving problems. You must be thinking that you want to become an entrepreneur to earn a living, not to solve someone's problems. However, solving problems is in fact, the thing that is going to make you an entrepreneur and earn a living.

Skills. Problems. Skills. Problems. Which comes first, the chicken or the egg? In this case, the problem will come before the skills. Any skill can be turned into a product or service that someone will be willing and happy to pay for.

In other words, we all have problems although we may not necessarily see them as such. Let's call them needs.

Everyone has a need or desire that they must fulfill and cannot do so themselves. This is where the problem and solution come in. What is in demand and there is not currently a product for? What service do they need accomplished and do not have the skill or desire to do so? Does someone want to create a blog but does not have the technical skill to set up the site? Does your friend want to learn to speak Spanish? How many women do you know who are looking for a skin care regimen?

The challenge is to convert the skills and passions that you have identified as uniquely your own into a product or service that someone will pay for. Your goal is to utilize the qualities that you possess to fulfill a need. You have 'it' and someone else wants it.

If you can do something better, faster, less expensively than anyone else, you have a product to offer. If you have an extraordinary skill, you have a service to offer. You have a gift that others are envious of and wish they could do, making you stand out from the rest. You are an entrepreneur.

Be the answer to someone's problem. Let's look at the list that you created and evaluate each item for its resolution capabilities. Don't skip over anything because you think that it would not be possible to earn any money from it. Even your hobbies can be turned into a cash machine. For each item, create a list of problems and how you may be able to use your skill to solve it.

Maybe you are handsome. Although you may not think this is a saleable item, maybe you could produce online courses about seduction. Maybe you are overweight. You could earn millions showing the world how much you eat (not recommended by the way). If you can write well, but don't want to publish a book with your own name, ghostwrite for someone else. Someone could be looking for an easier, faster way to scramble eggs and you have designed the perfect pan.

As you evaluate your skills, look at each with the intent of answering the question, "how can this skill be useful to people?" Online entrepreneurship is not about what you know or what you think you know. It is about how you are going to be the answer to a problem. From this point forward you should equate the phrase "what are my skills" with "what problem can I solve". When you understand this concept, you will have taken your first step towards starting your online business and becoming an entrepreneur.

You may have started reading this chapter thinking and believing that you did not have any inherent skills that you can use to start your online business or that you can solve a problem with. Even if that is still the case, know that there are still many opportunities available to you for you to be profitable. You can certainly take advantage of others' products and services to solve customers' problems. However, there are also many paths that you should NOT venture down. We will discuss some of these traps, scams and fraudulent opportunities in the next chapter.

Second part of the password to get the PDF: stay

The PDF summarizes the business assessments contained in this book, plus a list of extremely useful, online tools in a printable, **clickable**, handy, on-the-go version. Keep reading to find the next part of the Password at the end of the next Chapter.

But before you go on, if you enjoy reading this book, please take thirty seconds to **leave me a review**. Find the direct

All The links and tools listed in this book are available for free at www.emcpress.com in an easily clickable PDF File

link to the Amazon Review Page on the PDF you downloaded from **www.emcpress.com**. Thank you!

All The links and tools listed in this book are available for free at www.emcpress.com in an easily clickable PDF File

CHAPTER 3

ONLINE BUSINESS TO AVOID

"Business" is defined as commercial or industrial enterprise; dealings or transactions especially of an economic nature per the Merriam-Webster Dictionary[xi]. We have discussed that you want to be an entrepreneur and the skills required, now let's talk about business in itself and some things to avoid when it comes to starting your online business.

The key word in the definition of business is 'economic nature'. You should not be interested in engaging in any type of transaction or accepting any risk if it were not for profitable gain. Do not jump into a business venture that is less than reputable. Certainly, you would not enter into any business dealings simply for the short term. When discussing 'businesses' from this point forward, we will keep three goals in mind: sustainability, long-term and profitable.

Sustainability

Before you considered starting an online business, you probably did not have much use for the word sustainability. Sustainability is an approach to business that takes into consideration how it will survive although it is faced with challenges, and possibly roadblocks. It is the strategy that will carry it into the future and the long-term plans to handle the problems that will rear their ugly heads. You want to ensure that you are making decisions that are good, equitable, responsible and ethical based on sound reasoning and logic. This is not something that can occur without a plan.

A sustainable online business is not simply about having a great idea that you love. It is about thinking and planning into the future; developing a plan that will evolve as the market and competition evolves. It is not simply accepting that your business is successful and profitable in the moment but always considering the next step, the next move and future possibilities and challenges.

Developing a sustainable business begins with your mission. These are your values and how you will go about executing them. Your mission will capture what the ultimate goal of your online business is. The obvious answer to the question is to earn money. However, more importantly, consider what it is that you plan to accomplish by creating an online business. Back to the previous chapter, what problem are you hoping to solve? By defining your mission early on, you can then determine your objectives and your strategy as to how you will accomplish the things you have laid out in your mission.

Your mission statement is nothing but words if you have not created value around the mission. As we discussed in the last chapter, the value is the product or service that you will be offering or producing for your online customers. It is the thing that makes consumers WANT to buy your product or your service. Think of something that has value in your life. It does not have to be something expensive but it has to mean something to you. It should give you an emotional response and therefore make you believe it has more value than even the amount that you paid for it. Consider the handyman and the value that he provides to the busy entrepreneur. Although the repairs required to maintain your home may not cost a lot of money, the value is in the knowledge that the repairs are completed and your family is safe. This emotional response may be more valuable than that amount that you paid for the handyman's service.

Value of course, is all in the perception of the consumer. It is in the value or worth that you perceive the end result to have. Now consider how you are going to represent that value to your potential customer with the expectation that they will pay for it. This will be part of your business strategy.

Imagine producing an online video course. You love your idea; you produce the video and it is well received in the market, turning a profit. You think you are a success and that you have created a "successful" online business. You go out and buy a new car and enroll your son into a new, more expensive school because in your mind you have a long-term business. Suddenly, your competitor develops a better, more efficient, cheaper online course. Your video becomes obsolete and although it *was* profitable, it is no longer profitable nor sustainable. In other words, your "one hit wonder" did make you some money and it did provide you with an online business until it could no longer meet your requirements for long-term or profitable. The way that it was designed and marketed, it did NOT give you a sustainable opportunity for the long-term. Of course, the big question is then what could you do differently to make it sustainable. As you are developing your online course, plan for future courses as well. Develop your long-term strategy for managing foreseeable problems such as obsoletion and competitive pricing. Plan the next course while you are marketing the first one.

Creating a sustainable business, one which will continue to provide you with wealth for the long-term, requires planning and design. As an entrepreneur, your ability to think strategically and for the long-term will in turn bring you the profit and success that you are searching for.

Long-term

In terms of a business, long-term can be defined as a business that lasts a lifetime. It provides you with a standard of living and provides opportunity and wealth for your future generations. Depending upon your personal and entrepreneurial goals, the term 'long-term' may be different to everyone. Ask a child how long they have been waiting at the doctor's office. The answer will most certainly be 'an eternity'. The same question asked of an adult is probably more reasonably '5 minutes'. Each person, in various stages of life, will have a differing opinion on what long-term is and you have to decide for yourself. But in a business sense, you want your business to far exceed your lifetime and possibly be your legacy.

If you are willing to put in the effort, and you definitely will need to put in the effort, this should be the ultimate goal of your online business. You should develop a business that will survive the market and its competitors; the ups and downs of supply and demand; the fluctuations in market needs, demands and consumer desires. Your time and energy are extremely valuable resources that should not be wasted on anything that will not produce a positive outcome for you either in the near future or in preparation for the long-term. Whatever opportunity that does not meet the requirements of sustainable and long-term should not be considered as a business.

Profitable

Just because you are starting a business does not mean that it will automatically be profitable. Like in any business venture, there are costs associated with start-up of an online business. "Online" simply means that the sales channel is on the Internet versus a standard brick and mortar establishment. Of course, there are costs associated with an online business as well, but hopefully significantly less. To define a business as profitable, it should be financially beneficial to you. Aside from start-up costs and regular maintenance expenses, your online business should in fact, be putting money into your pocket versus a constant drain on your wallet.

The fact that you decided to START a business is not going to automatically make you rich. There are a large number of factors and inputs that will determine if your product or service makes you any money and we will go into this in later chapters. What you need to decide as you set out to begin your online business is how will you measure whether the business that you create will give you the profit or income that you are looking for.

With these three goals in mind, we will now look at businesses that do NOT qualify as viable online businesses because they do not meet the criteria we expect of sustainable, long-term and profitable. We'll also discuss the risks of beginning an online business in general.

Scams

Over the last few years, scams and short-cuts have popped up on the Internet, enticing the unsuspecting, motivated entrepreneur. They have gotten traction because inevitably, someone out there will attempt it, thinking it will make them rich, or bring them closer to their goal. In fact, there are probably millions of people who fall victim to the fraudulent "business" ideas and ventures that tempt those unsuspecting, hungry entrepreneurs. However, you will NOT become a statistic; one of millions who is sold a bill of goods or an idea that is supposed to make them an instant millionaire.

The expression "If it looks too good to be true, it probably is" seems a bit pessimistic but in fact, it is a good way to check reality. If a deal, promotion or online business opportunity looks too good to be true, be wary. It is probably a scam, with the scammer trying to obtain your personal information, to persuade you to buy something that doesn't actually exist, or worse. There are many signs to look for to determine if an opportunity is possibly a scam and we will touch on a few here. If you suspect that you are being scammed, move on!

- Earning money online will require effort no matter what the business is. If any proposal or opportunity guarantees you a level of income or profit, it is probably a scam. Unless you are employed by a company and offered a salary, there are no guarantees whatsoever when it comes to online businesses. There are too many factors involved such as market, product, marketing, timing, pricing, etc. for any promises to be made about your earning potential.

- As discussed, there will be expenses associated with starting your online business. However, if you are asked to "send money" without the intent of buying a product or service, it is probably a scam.

- Nothing in life is Free. Everything comes at a price, especially when it comes to business. Everyone is out there to earn money and if something is offered for FREE, be conscious that there will probably be something that follows; some request, demand or suggestion that if you pay, you will get to the next level or receive some special concession.

- Here today, gone tomorrow. This applies to fraudulent and deceptive businesses, but if it is legitimate, it will be available whether you decide today or tomorrow or next week to take the next step. If the proposal is telling you to "act fast, offer expires tonight", be careful of getting sucked into this scam.

- Earn money overnight. Be realistic. Although we all can dream about earning a large sum of money from very little effort, the reality is that it will take hard work, time and energy to earn money from an online business. If an opportunity touts that you can earn cash fast, run even faster. Slow and steady wins the race!

- Big Money. The thrill of earning a huge paycheck is appealing to just about everyone. Who wouldn't get excited about the opportunity of earning a large sum of money from doing virtually NOTHING! Buyer beware!

From unrealistic expectations to lofty goals, a scam business will make you feel like you can achieve ANYTHING, to only set you up to fail! Don't get scammed! If the business opportunity online looks suspicious, be cautious and investigate. Do your homework! As we progress through the next pages, exploring online business opportunities that may NOT be viable options for you or those that you should avoid at all cost, keep three questions in mind: Is it sustainable? Is it for the long-term? Is it profitable?

Mystery Shopper

If you have discovered through your skills evaluation that your friends come to you often for fashion tips and in fact, you love shopping, an opportunity to be a mystery shopper sounds appealing. Marketing and research companies hire you to visit local stores, purchase product and provide information about the buying and shopping experience. In the best-case scenario, you as the shopper will receive some form of payment for your services.

Although there are legitimate opportunities out there with companies who will pay you to be a mystery shopper, there are others who are simply running a scam. Never, ever PAY a fee to register as a mystery shopper or to obtain any type of training or certification. If you are asked to pay, this will be your indication that it is a scam.

If you are serious about taking advantage of mystery shopping as a business, do your research. Identify mystery shopping companies that accept applications online and thoroughly research them. Accept shopping assignments only when you are confident and comfortable that the opportunity is legitimate.

Now let's go back and look at our definition of a business and more importantly, a successful online business. As we discussed early on, there are certain qualities which will help you in your quest to become an entrepreneur. One of these, curiosity, must be ever-present as you begin this part of the entrepreneurial journey. Asking 'why', 'how' and 'what if' will help you to avoid making some mistakes early on that may prevent you from succeeding later on or in this venture at all.

First, let's look at whether an online business as a mystery shopper is a sustainable business idea. Does it solve a problem that you can develop a mission statement and strategy around? Will it offer you enough opportunity to meet your long-term goals? Will it provide you with the income that you are looking for? These are just some of the many questions that you should ask yourself about the opportunity as a Mystery Shopper. In all likelihood, the answer is NO to all of these and you should NOT consider it as a viable option for an online business. It is definitely NOT a business that you should get in to.

Multi-Level Marketing

Pyramid Schemes have been around for generations. Similar to a pyramid scheme, multi-level marketing requires you to go into your address book, or now a days, your Facebook friends list and LinkedIn Connections to ask people to not only purchase the product, but to join you in your mission. For each person that you recruit, you earn a portion of commission and additional money on their recruiting and sales. Aside from the fact that you typically have to PAY to receive your kit, your products or your marketing plan, Pyramid schemes are in fact, illegal!

Call it a pyramid scheme, a Ponzi scheme or multi-level marketing, the concept behind it is that each member of the network takes a piece of the pie. The limiting factor is that there are just not enough people in the world or in the network for it to be beneficial to anyone except those at the top. The difference between each is that in multi-level marketing, there is actually a product to sell. It can be argued that multi-level marketing is simply a legalized pyramid scheme. If your earning potential is in any way tied to your ability to recruit others to join your team, you can be pretty sure that it falls into this category. There is always some form of deception or fraud involved in either the marketing or even the sale of the product. Even those that may seem legitimate, still attract potential 'business partners' through some form of deception; promise of a huge income, fast way to earn cash, great way to meet people. Ultimately, all of these types of marketing strategies fail.

Those companies that market this type of business do a wonderful job at making it *look* like a legitimate business opportunity. From the website to the marketing material to the potential income, the business appears to be reasonable, logical and legal. According to the Federal Trade Commission, "It's best not to get involved in plans where the money you make is based primarily on the number of distributors you recruit and your sales to them, rather than on your sales to people outside the plan who intend to use the products."[xii]

This is not to say that ALL multi-level marketing programs are fraudulent or intentionally deceptive. There are some indicators though that the opportunity may require additional research:

- Is the product something that you would actually support? This is a big one. If the product or service is not reputable or is just plain old junk, do not risk your reputation by getting involved with it. Of course, you want to represent a company and product that you believe in and would use yourself. If you have to stretch the truth about its value or worthiness, this should raise some concern about the product's validity as well.

- Promise of a huge income. As we have discussed, your online business is going to require effort. A legitimate business cannot make guarantees of the earning potential right out of the gate. Instant success and a huge profit are very rare in this type of market and you should be skeptical.

- Target Market. In a multi-level marketing structure, you should be selling a product or service to the end-user. If the description of the opportunity indicates that you will be selling to other distributors, be wary. Shuffling sales between distributors sounds very shady to say the least.

- Bulletin Board Ad. If you saw an advertisement on a bulletin board at the supermarket, it would be responsible of you as an entrepreneur and future business owner to do your homework. Aside from dog-walking and odd-jobs, there are not many opportunities that would pan out for you in the way that you want if you find it in a community bulletin.

Research. Research. If you are considering participating in any type of multi-level marketing, be sure that you have done your homework. Is it a reputable company with a valuable product to offer? Has anyone that you know heard of the product or business? Would you buy it yourself?

Remember the three goals that we want to keep in mind as we evaluate online business opportunities. Sustainable, long-term and profitable. Evaluate how a multi-level marketing business would hold up when we look at this through this lens. Consider how many people could you reasonably recruit to join you on this journey and how would your network sustain the ability to keep the business up and running for the long-term. The possibility of actually making money if you are dependent upon your ability and that of others to convert people into believers as well is slim to none.

This leads to other questions: How many of your friends and family would simply buy the product or join the business out of pity for you? Do you really want your income to be limited by the number of people you can convince that this is a genuine, viable business? Looking at this business "opportunity" closely, it does not appear that multi-level marketing would be a good option for an online business for you and is definitely NOT a business.

Binary Options Trading

Like many people, you may never have heard of a binary trading option. Similar to day trading, a binary option is dependent on the outcome of a yes/no market proposition. [xiii] In other words, a binary options trader will make either a fixed profit or a fixed loss. Unlike day trading, there are no other factors other than yes or no involved in the purchase or sale of an asset. Assets are not bought and sold for the actual price but rather a value between zero and 100. This is probably the riskiest of all online businesses.

Although there is a lot of money to be earned in binary options trading and it is a legitimate opportunity for someone, if you are looking to fix your financial problems overnight, this is certainly not the way to do it. In fact, this is one of the ways that scammers will try to convince you that it is a wise business opportunity. A bogus website promises that for an initial deposit of several hundred dollars, you can quickly earn thousands by doing virtually nothing. You then are asked to "invest" heavily to increase your income possibilities. In theory, binary options trading is more about luck than using any of the skills that we have determined are required to be an entrepreneur or more importantly, the skills that you possess.

It is true that you can earn some money by choosing yes or no on the movement of certain assets in the market. But it is not a business that will provide you with a sustainable, long-term business that will provide your family with wealth for future generations. We know based on the trading market that the earning potential is there. However, if you are interested in reaching the goals as we have previously discussed, earning a living by becoming an entrepreneur and creating a brand and market for yourself, then binary options trading is not the online business that will be right for you.

Gambling and Betting

It is important to note that as of November, 2018, only four states in the U.S. currently legally permit online gambling (Delaware, Nevada, New Jersey and Pennsylvania). That being said, it is illegal in all other states across the country. This should stop you in your tracks. However, if it does not and you are still looking into the possibility of online gambling for your entrepreneurial debut, keep reading.

Gambling is NOT a business. By definition, gambling is the risk of losing something important by taking a chance on something else. Of course, beginning an online or brick and mortar business is a risk no matter the industry or marketplace. You are starting a business for long-term sustainability and profit, not a get rich quick solution. Again, online gambling is illegal in the majority of states and you can be faced with legal issues if you engage in this type of "business". Do not allow your desire to become an entrepreneur override your sense of morals and ethics and possibly jeopardize your future instead of improve it.

Basing a long-term business opportunity on risk alone is a recipe for disaster. Some gamblers claim to have a "lucky streak", earning them thousands, if not millions, of dollars. Sure, you may turn a profit from your investments, but it could be at a significant cost to you both personally and professionally. Hopefully this discussion has convinced you that online gambling and betting is NOT a viable business option.

Work-from-Home

If you are reading this book, it is clear that you want to be an entrepreneur, managing your own time and resources, not working for "the man" any longer. This desire is more and more prominent as people are looking for some extra cash; large companies are down-sizing, leaving many without jobs; those in mid-life are looking for a career change. Whatever your reasoning behind wanting to start your own business, know that you are not alone and that is why and how so many opportunities have come about over the years to work-at-home.

The theory of supply and demand is the economic model defining at what point the need for a product and the availability of the product meet. As more and more people have the desire for something (demand), the more opportunities spring up to meet that need (supply). With a greater percentage of the population around the world interested in purchasing goods and services online (demand), the more opportunities (supply) that exist for online businesses and entrepreneurs to sell them what they are looking for.

Unfortunately, scammers and frauds have jumped on the band wagon as well as we've seen, looking for the convenient way to earn a living versus the good old-fashioned way of earning it legitimately through hard work, persistence and skill. Work-at-home opportunities can be seen in any type of industry you can think of; from medical billing to stuffing envelopes to telemarketing scams. As of 2011, work-from-home scams topped the list of Internet crimes.[xiv] Since then scammers have gotten more sophisticated, giving the unsuspecting entrepreneur more things to watch out for, including some of the following:

- You are contacted via email or social media with an offer for a work-from-home opportunity. If you receive some type of communication like this, be sure to do your research. Although some opportunities may be legitimate, be mindful if you didn't contact the company directly.

- No phone interviews. If you are asked to communicate strictly via chat or email, ask to have a phone interview. Do not leave something as important as starting a business to interpretation via a tiny chat window only.

- Send us money $$ so you can get started right away. Although it may seem reasonable that you will have to make some type of investment in your online business venture, giving someone your banking information would be just irresponsible and sending money without having fully researched the opportunity would be foolish.

- Suspicious website. When you enter a search in Google, you are more than likely going to find multiple websites that appear to be very similar to the one that you were expecting or looking for. Scammers have gotten very creative in the naming of their fake websites, assuming that naïve and unsuspecting victims will not notice the slight variation. This is how they get you. They make you believe that you are applying for an opportunity on a legitimate business website, only to be duped into some type of scam.

During your research and evaluation of work-from-home opportunities, always keep our three goals in mind: sustainable, long-term and profitable. Let's look at this more closely with an envelope-stuffing business. The idea of stuffing envelopes may seem like a viable opportunity and it very well may be with a little ingenuity. However, as the digital world expands, the quantity of envelopes has and will continue to decrease. According to The Boston

Consulting Group in a study about mail volumes, it is projected that the volume of mail that passes through the postal system will drastically decline over the next several years, from a high volume of 213 billion pieces in 2006 to a projected 150 billion by 2020.[xv] This does not set up an envelope stuffing business as a sustainable business for the long-term.

Although we have discussed here many fraudulent, risky and illegal business opportunities that you may come across on the Internet, understand that there are also many others that are simply unethical or immoral. You be the judge as to how you interpret what may be qualified as shady or nefarious. From a business practice perspective though, anything that could possibly be dangerous or detrimental to humans, animals or the environment would be considered as an unethical business practice.[xvi] Of course there are other types of unethical behavior and practices involving pricing, competition, marketing and employment.

As you consider the online business opportunity that you will embark on, bear in mind the potential risks and consequences of engaging in any of these types of businesses. There are so many inherent risks of operating an online business including financial risk; technological exposure such as hacking; legal vulnerability from patents, trademarks and copyrights. There is no need to subject yourself or your business to other liabilities. The online marketplace, while it can be profitable, sustainable and bring long-term success for many, it also opens the door to a plethora of dangerous and uncertain opportunities. As the saying goes, "Buyer Beware". This applies not only to the consumer but anyone engaging in any type of transaction on the Internet.

Now that we have examined many opportunities which appear less than ideal for you, the entrepreneur, let's now identify where the money actually lies behind the screen of your laptop and how you can take advantage of these opportunities with some of the skills that you already possess.

Third part of the password to get the PDF: intouch

The PDF summarizes the business assessments contained in this book, plus a list of extremely useful, online tools in a printable, **clickable**, handy, on-the-go version. Keep reading to find the next part of the Password at the end of the next Chapter.

But before you go on, if you enjoy reading this book, please take thirty seconds to **leave me a review**. Find the direct link to the Amazon Review Page on the PDF you downloaded from **www.emcpress.com**. Thank you!

CHAPTER 4

REAL AND VIABLE ONLINE BUSINESSES

It should be obvious by now that we are primarily targeting online businesses as the basis of this book. Of course, all of the rules and theories apply to any business or entrepreneur. Because this book is focused on online businesses, it should not be necessary to over emphasize the Internet and more importantly, a website. However, let's go there anyway.

In its earliest stage in the 1990's, the Internet was responsible for approximately 1% of the world's communication. By 2007, more than 97% of global telecommunication occurred via the Internet.[xvii] Developed in 1989 by Tim Berners-Lee, the World Wide Web has become what we all use today as part of the system of websites and webpages and which most of us can no longer live without. Most people don't even remember the days BEFORE you could Google anything you wanted. You had to actually go to the library to do any research or pick up a newspaper and search the Help Wanted section to find a new job.

The World Wide Web has changed the world forever; a fact that has created millions of jobs and opportunities for people around the world. It is also the source of fraud, deception, theft and disappointment. It is how you use the Internet and the information that can be obtained that will determine whether you are one of the successful ones or unfortunately, one of the victims. As someone interested in creating and growing an online business, it is important to understand that the Internet is a very powerful tool and resource and for you, will become a source of income.

So, let's look at some types of online businesses that are in fact, real and viable online businesses. For each, we will discuss some of the required skills, hopefully some of which you possess based on your evaluation; training opportunities; the passiveness index; the expected investment if necessary; earning potential; and risks if any.

By the end of this book, it is my goal that you will be ready to go and start your own online business.

Amazon FBA

Of course, you have heard of Amazon and its worldwide fulfillment networks. Fulfillment by Amazon, or FBA, is a platform designed to assist you with managing your business more effectively. Rather than you having to manage your own inventory and shipping for each sale, Amazon will do it for you. Having built its business on customer service, you can be certain that your product is not only in good hands, but since all shipping and returns is handled through Amazon, your customers will receive the same amazing service and delivery that all Amazon customers receive.

The FBA program offers business owners the flexibility of selling their own brand and products with the security, visibility and reliability behind the Amazon name and reputation. So, as amazing as this opportunity sounds, let's talk about how you get started.

As with starting any business, the first step in creating an online business is to research. Of course, your goal is to find a profitable niche of products that will provide a sustainable, long-term business opportunity for you to create wealth for your future generations. There are however, many things to take into consideration when considering the niche such as training, certifications, sourcing and manufacturing, and customs.

Amazon FBA offers you the opportunity to reach millions of customers with your product from the comfort of your home. Now, this is not to say that it will necessarily be any easier than having a brick and mortar business, but at least your inventory, shipping and customer service will be managed for you. Now let's get started on the research.

In the beginning of this book, you looked at your skills and passions and hopefully you have a working list at this time. To start researching what niche to target for FBA, first look at those products that you are most interested in. You may try using the keyword finder through Google to identify some things that are searched for often by using a tool at www.kwfinder.com. For example, if you are passionate about tools you may want to start your research in this area to determine if it would even be worth it for you to move forward, depending upon profitability.

What types of tools are customers buying on Amazon? What qualities do they want in a product and what price point are they willing to buy it at? As you are doing your research, you need to keep a few things in mind:

- Few competitors selling this type of product.

- Existing demand. Customers are buying existing and/or similar products.

- Product is missing the mark on customer's expectations. There are many products which may be selling well on Amazon, yet customer reviews indicated that there is some deficiency or quality issue with the product.

- Legal. Steer clear of any products that have a patent, or are risky for safety reasons. Regulated items are definitely an area that you should avoid such as alcohol, safety equipment and medical devices.

Looking closer at this concept of customers' expectations, there is a huge opportunity for you to be creative and utilize your existing skills in this area. Customers are very quick to review products more often when they are dissatisfied than when they are in fact happy with the product. By reviewing what customers are saying about an existing product, you have the opportunity make it better, to improve its qualities and make it more appealing to the customer. Here is where the competitive advantage comes in. You are not developing the design from scratch, but rather making improvements to an already existing product.

Like with your self-evaluation, researching products to sell through FBA will require you to think outside of the box. Your gut reaction is probably to identify products that are selling well and are popular. In fact, we are suggesting quite the opposite. You should be identifying products that may not be as popular or have great potential if marketed properly. Here are some tips to help you look at products:

- Evaluate products on Amazon that are interesting or unique. There may be a niche market here that you can capitalize on.

- Look at products which only a few vendors are selling and then evaluate the total number of sales. If only a few vendors are selling more than 2,000 units per month, this may be a product that meets your specifications and may be worthy of further investigation.

- Scrutinize the number of stars that a product receives. If it is a 3.5 or higher, there probably is not much room for improvement and customers are fairly satisfied with it.

- Be sure to keep notes as you do your research to identify any trends, things that catch your eye or pricing and product information. You never know when you may stumble on a piece of information or a possible grand slam on a product. You may even be able to identify a product or idea based on something else you saw in your research.

- Read reviews. Just because a product may be selling well, does not mean that customers are actually satisfied with it. This may be the perfect opportunity to be creative, taking an existing product and its poor qualities or characteristics and turn it into something that customers will not only want but will love.

Now that you have a product in your sights, here is where the brainstorming comes in. Once you have read all of the reviews, you should have a fairly good idea as to what the customers like and more importantly, don't like about the product. How can you change a negative comment to a positive one? What quality adjustment will make the customers happy? Of course, successfully implementing the changes will be determined by the manufacturing facility that you choose to utilize for the product, but you should be prepared to have all of your improvement suggestions ready so that when you move to the next step, the process goes much smoother.

At this point, I am sure you are thinking, "where in the world do I go now to find someone to make this thing for me?" It is actually much simpler than you might think. There is a large company in China whose mission is to help people like you to sell and distribute products around the world. By doing a simple search at **www.alibaba.com**, you can easily identify a host of factories that may be producing a similar product and may be willing to work with you to produce yours as well. Although this may seem overwhelming at first, by sending a few emails you can easily narrow down your search to just a few companies. Then, by asking the right questions, you can get a better understanding of the process, how you can work together and answers to some very key questions such as pricing, lead time, packaging and shipping. If a potential supplier is able to answer your questions in a timely fashion and with ease, this may be a good opportunity to discuss your ideas further.

Of course, the potential manufacturer will not be able to provide you with much detail about packaging, labeling or even pricing until you provide them with some key information as well such as who you are and what it is you would like to produce and how many units you are expecting. Then the real negotiations begin.

This may be a scary step when you are considering that you will be working with people that you do not know, in a country that you are not familiar with and with whom you are placing your trust to provide you with a product that will in the end be profitable. This is the point where many online entrepreneurs get cold feet. Using your leadership and entrepreneurial skills that you already have or are developing, I am certain that you too can make the negotiations happen.

From the research stage, to negotiations to labeling and shipping and even customs clearance and taxes, you will have a lot to learn. This process will not happen overnight and may in fact, require several months from start to finish. There are many risks involved and out of all of the online business opportunities, managing an Amazon FBA business may be the most difficult. However, that does not mean it is impossible nor does it mean that it is out of *your* reach. You may be thinking right now, "why would I want to go through all of this trouble? Or can I really earn a living from Amazon FBA sales?" The answers to these questions of course are "to create a sustainable, long-term and profitable business and YES". Yes, you can earn a very nice living from the program with diligence, persistence and hard work.

All of the above information is presented to you assuming that you will be improving a product that is currently available. However, your FBA selling account does not have to be that complicated. You can even begin by selling items that you already own or make. The point though is that you must do your research. You do not want to send inventory to Amazon for them to ship and provide customer service for if you know it won't sell, may be out of date or simply irrelevant. To ensure a successful online business, it is crucial for you to do your homework.

Some of the profitable niche markets that have already been identified which may be worth considering for your own business include:

- Before calling a contractor or vendor, many people rely on videos to attempt to do-it themselves. DIY supplies are very popular and are proving to be very profitable for those who have jumped on the band wagon.

- As parents and educators become more and more concerned about educating our youth, educational kits have become a popular investment and opportunity for an online business.

- Analysts predict that gardening tools will be in greater demand as more and more people are passionate about their gardens and yards.

- If you have ever traveled by air, you know that luggage is not necessarily handled with loving care. Travelers are looking to not only protect their luggage but differentiate it from the millions of others like it with luggage protectors. These low-cost items can earn a very nice profit online for an entrepreneur.

- The pet industry is booming as people's pets become more like family. Retractable dog leashes are the latest in pet products and are making a very nice profit for sellers of this product.

Now that you have a basic understanding of what Fulfillment by Amazon is and how you can get involved, let's look at some key indicators and the reality of it all:

TOOLS:

KWFINDER (MUST: Keywords research)

ALIBABA (all the Chinese suppliers for FBA)

JUNGLE SCOUT (MUST: Niche finder and products evaluation)

AMZTracker (Tools for Amazon Sellers)

CAMELCAMEL (Price Tracker)

- **Required skills**. An entrepreneurial spirit, a passion and desire to be successful, and of course, curiosity. However, these will be required for each and every opportunity that you pursue. Let's be real, the skills that you really need include online research, creativity to invent or improve products and marketing.

- **Training and Learning curve**: High. Many people will give up early in this venture because it will not be easy. You will need to learn how to research products, identify suppliers if necessary, shipping and customs regulations, trade laws. There are many online courses, videos and blogs available that will teach you how to start an online FBA business such as

    o https://services.amazon.com/tutorials-and-training.htm

- https://www.bigcommerce.com/blog/amazon-seller-account-checklist/#common-amazon-seller-faqs
- https://www.nchannel.com/blog/how-to-sell-on-amazon-for-beginners-using-fba/
- https://www.junglescout.com/blog/category/the-million-dollar-case-study/

- **Passiveness Index**: Low. Initially you will have to put a lot of effort into research and establishing the business with no return on your investment. Once products are in inventory at an Amazon fulfillment center, this business will still require daily interaction and engagement with customers.

- **Investment**: The initial investment to create your Amazon FBA account will be minimal, less than $50 depending upon the program you select. Any other investment will be based upon the products that you sell and the supplier you select (manufacturer of new product or distributor of existing). Also, there will be fees paid to Amazon for shipping and customer services.

- **Reasonable monthly goal in one year**: $1000 - $5000 per month once your product or products are available.

- **Risks**: Negative reviews. Just as you found negative reviews helpful in your research, customers could also leave negative reviews about your product. Amazon could possibly lose inventory. High customer return rate. Amazon undercutting and selling similar products. Manufacturing and shipping issues.

The Amazon FBA business opportunity is certainly a good and viable business but it will require effort, diligence and research. It is not a get-rich quick opportunity.

Self-Publishing on Amazon

Maybe through your evaluation and skills assessment you have discovered that you really want to write a book. No reason to stop with just one. Self-publishing can be a very viable business, earning you a very nice living. As per our evaluation of online businesses suggests, it would qualify as a sustainable, long-term and profitable business. It may be hard to conceive but let's take a look at an example.

Mark Dawson, a UK-based author of thrillers and crime novels, earns $450,000 per year on Amazon with his self-published books according to Forbes magazine.[xviii] Although it seems unbelievable, know that Mark started out with nothing and even experienced rejection and failure. This is part of the entrepreneur's journey and as we already discussed, should not be feared as long as you learn from your mistakes. Clearly, Mark Dawson learned from his mistakes and came back to earn an astounding figure, and more than likely changed the long-term trajectory of his life and that of his future generations. This is where we all want to be and self-publishing is certainly one way to get there.

Self-publishing is vastly different from traditional publishing as you may know it. Of course, it is every author's dream to be represented by a traditional publisher, yet very few published authors earn a living this way. According to Jane Friedman, a writing and publishing expert, "70 percent of authors do not earn out their advance."[xix] So, if you have the desire and the writing ability, don't be discouraged if you are not one of the few to get an advance and be restricted and controlled. Go out and do your own thing.

The self-publishing industry is very hot right now and with its popularity, it makes you wonder what the future is for traditional publishers. Self-published authors have the responsibility to not only write the material or content, but to publish in a format that will be desirable to the public. Even this term, desirable, raises some question. What does today's reader want? Are they looking for hard cover books, e-books that they can read on their phone or device, blog posts, articles? The world of self-publishing has opened tremendous opportunities for people of all walks of life, creativity levels and even for an infinite number of topics.

If you do a simple search on Google about something you are passionate about, you are sure to come across hundreds, if not thousands, of websites about your topic. The term *author* is no longer limited to only those few writers who have been deemed worthy of the attention, the press and notoriety offered by large publication companies. The Stephen Kings and J.K. Rawlings of the world are few and far between compared to the number of people who are now self-publishing their work on the Internet. If you write an article, blog or book, you are technically considered the author and because you make it available for the public to view, you are by default, a self-published author.

With self-publishing, you have many benefits over traditional publishing. You have control of the content, the timing, the product description, the marketing and even the pricing whereas a traditional publishing firm will control all of this for you. If you are not interested in maintaining control of the product, not concerned about how it is marketed or how your target audience receives it, then maybe the traditional publishing route is better suited for you. Bringing your content to the world in a way that you want it delivered will certainly require more work and effort but it will give you the satisfaction in knowing that you have control over how it is presented to your audience.

Of course, self-publishing any material will not be easy. But, if you treat your writing like a business, which is the substance of this book, then writing and publishing your work can be a very profitable venture. In fact, many authors have taken that leap of faith, leaving their careers or jobs to focus solely on their writing business.

Let's jump in and see what it will take to become a self-published author on Amazon and then you decide for yourself if this will be a viable online business for you. No matter the format that you will choose to make the content available, book, e-book, audiobook, etc., the steps will be the same to launch your online business.

- Research. Research. Research. As we talked about earlier, a large amount of research is necessary before you begin any business venture. Do a keyword search on Google to find out what things people are reading. When it comes to self-publishing, you want to write what people want to read. Your material will be uniquely yours, but it needs to be relevant to your target audience. Writing about things that people want to read is the first step towards becoming successful in your niche market.

  There are quite a few websites out there geared towards readers. If you are writing fiction or non-fiction books, research what is popular, what is trending and what is on everyone's "to be read lists". Amazon has a great tool that tells you what books others have purchased or are reading. By doing your research, you can identify what topics are hot and where you have the greatest opportunity to profit. You are not getting into the self-publishing business to reinvent the wheel, creating a new and unique genre of books. Take advantage of existing trends and jump right in.

- Write. Write content that your readers will talk about with other people. You don't want to be a one-hit-wonder, only writing one book or e-book, but rather find that niche that will sustain your business for the long-term. Through your research, write about what the audience wants to read, while adding your own unique twists, characters, thoughts and voice.

- Quality and quantity. As you are writing your first piece of work to be published, be sure to think about the next. Of course, you don't want to produce junk, so take your time. But you also want to capture your audience's attention, preparing them for the next book, the next article. Grab their attention with the quality of your work and then give them what they want with the quantity.

- Repeat the process. Once you have the idea and the content, don't stop there. Have the next book ready to go even before the first one is published. It is hard enough to gain a new customer or get them interested in your work. When you grab their attention, you want to keep them before they lose interest and move on to someone else.

You now have your amazing content, and you know your target audience because you have done your research. You are now ready to publish on Amazon! The next thing you need to do is put your best foot forward and have a cover designed that best represents your work and is eye-catching to your audience. They say that a picture is worth a thousand words. Some people may bypass your book as they are scrolling through hundreds of other books in this area simply because the cover is not appealing. Make it stand out, separate it from the pack and give yourself a head start towards reaching your goals.

Just because you have written an amazing story or are providing helpful information, does not mean that your audience will know what you are trying tell them. You must have an awesome description to draw your reader in and get them to buy. This is where you will have to take off your author's hat for a moment, and put on your marketing hat. Give the reader juicy nuggets of information, or leave them salivating, hungry to read the entire story. Read the descriptions of the top sellers in your genre or niche and learn how they capture their audience's attention through the description of their books as well.

Now you have to get the word out about your book. Self-published authors like Mark Dawson, Martin Crosbie and Jim Krukal will tell you that it takes hard work and dedication to write the book but then the true work begins when it comes to marketing. You cannot just assume that "if you build it, they will come". There are a variety of resources available to you online to give you insight into how to go from just a self-published author to possibly becoming one of the top independent authors on Amazon. Webinars, videos, online courses and podcasts are out there in abundance, helping you to navigate the self-publishing world, guaranteeing that you are reaching a wider audience and sharing your work worldwide.

Competition is high on Amazon with everyone vying for a piece of the proverbial pie. With more than six million e-book titles currently available and new ones being uploaded every few minutes, your work must stand out and you will need to work hard to do so. Writing and publishing on Amazon is certainly a viable business opportunity, but in order to ensure a sustainable and long-term business, you are going to have to diversify your writing as well. There are so many opportunities to get your work out there and in fact, create multiple streams of income for yourself, strengthening your business strategy. Audiobooks, blogs and even videos about your book will all help you to generate buzz around your work and your reputation as an author and improve your chances of building and sustaining a profitable online business as a self-published author.

Let's look at this idea of audiobooks a little more. As the world moves more and more to a digital platform, people want more access to things quickly and easily. For many, having a book read to them may be the only option that they have to read a book. Our busy, everyday lives make multi-tasking almost a necessity, so adding an audiobook to the list of things that we can accomplish while mowing the lawn or driving to work has become the norm. Even converting your book to an audio file has become easier with companies like ACX helping you to not only have it recorded but to publish it on all of the major sites such as Amazon, Audible.com and iTunes.

Before we move on, we have not considered the possibility that you do not have the skills or experience to actually write content. There are people out there in the depths of the Internet who love to and are capable of writing, but may not want the responsibility of publishing and marketing. These freelancers are willing to write content for you with no recognition or acknowledgement on the finished work. Just because you cannot do it yourself does not mean that you cannot develop an online business by outsourcing the writing process to one if not many freelancer writers.

Let's now look at some facts about the self-publishing business:

TOOLS:

JUNGLE SCOUT (MUST: Niche finder and products evaluation)

KDSPY (MUST: Niche finder and products evaluation)

PUBLISHER ROCKET (MUST: usefull tool for keywords and niches)

UPWORK (freelances marketplace better for ghostwriters)

FIVERR (freelances marketplace for ghostwriters, cover designers and so on)

GRAMMARLY (Simplifies writing)

BOOK REVIEW TARGETER (Find reviewers for your book)

- **Required skills**. Ability to write or find and hire a freelancer to write on your behalf. Online research to identify the niche or genre.

- **Training and Learning curve**: Medium. To be successful, you need to educate yourself about the self-publishing environment, what type of content readers are looking for and how to best market to your target audience. There are many articles, videos and blog posts available online to help you get started with your business venture including:

    - https://www.amazon.com/gp/seller-account/mm-summary-page.html?topic=200260520

    - www.Acx.com

- **Passiveness Index**: High. Self-publishing offers you the opportunity to be earning passive income regularly. As you have heard, once something is out there on the Internet, it stays there forever. Customers can continue to purchase your materials long after you have stopped marketing it or have moved on to another book.

- **Investment**: Little to none. Since you can create your account on Amazon KDP for no charge, you will not incur any expenses to create and upload your books and e-books. Of course, if you pay a ghostwriter or cover designer you will have those expenses but they will be minimal.

- **Reasonable monthly goal in one year**: Average of $5000 per month for established self-published authors; $50 per month for first time publishers.

- **Risks**: Writing is usually a solo endeavor and can become lonely. If your book is not selling as you had hoped, it can be discouraging and may seem like a failed attempt. But, keep at it. Since there is very little outlay, there are few financial risks associated with self-publishing.

As markets change and interests change, consider revisiting what it is that your readers will want to read. Keep your audience engaged, interested and always eager for your next book or audiobook to become available. By diversifying your content offerings, you can develop a successful online self-publishing business which will in fact, be profitable and sustainable for the long-term.

Ghostwriting

As mentioned in the previous chapter, hiring a ghostwriter is certainly an option when considering an online business in self-publishing. However, if you are not interested in the publishing side of the business but have identified that you have skills in writing, you have other options available to you to develop your online business.

The world revolves around words; words in various formats and meanings. It is what you do with them that determines your earning capability. With the Internet's huge impact on the world and virtually everything being put in writing, the writing opportunities are boundless and unending. There will always be someone who has something to say yet who lacks the ability to put words on paper, or in this case, on the computer. As we talked about earlier with the concept of supply and demand, the demand for things to be written can only be handled when there are people willing to write.

As an online business, ghostwriting can be profitable, sustainable and long-term with the constant flow and requirement of work to be completed. Depending on your skills, passions and desire, you will certainly be able to find a profitable niche market to write for. In this highly-technical, digital world that we are exploring, and as new entrepreneurs come onto the scene, there will be a greater demand for these writing and even editing skills to help out your fellow entrepreneurs.

Let's look at some steps to get you started as a ghostwriter:

The age-old question of "which came first, the chicken or the egg", seems to apply here. You want clients to hire you to write for them but you don't have anything to show them your writing skills. Without samples to show them, it may be difficult to get clients because they have no way of knowing what you are capable of, your writing style or your tone. This is a bit tricky when you are just starting out in the writing business. To combat this, try writing a few things on your own first. Since there are so many avenues and media where you can publish your own works, it should not be difficult to get something out to the public that you can then refer others to look at.

For example,

- Blog posts – if you don't yet have your own blog, reach out to others who do and offer to write articles for them. These are typically 500 – 1000-word posts that will at least give you some credibility.

- Articles – contact magazines in a specific niche area and offer to write articles for them. If for example, you are interested in fly fishing, contact the magazine that you possibly subscribe to and suggest a topic or subject and write about it for them. Having your name and article published in a reputable magazine will help substantiate your skills as well as give you a sense of what type of market you may be interested in writing for.

- Books – If creativity, plot and character development are right up your alley, try writing a fiction book. You will not be able to effectively ghostwrite for another author in this genre if you are not familiar with the organization and flow of a fictional book if you have never written one. Maybe if the creative juices aren't flowing like that, give your hand a try at writing a non-fiction book in an area of interest.

Once you have some material out there on your own, it will be easier to attract clients to your website to ghostwrite for them. There are literally dozens of avenues for your writing abilities and it all goes back to your skills evaluation that we discussed earlier. Some ghostwriters focus on only non-fiction books or memoirs. Others may write fiction books and stories. In the business world, clients may hire you to write articles, blog posts and business case studies. There is a huge market for copyrighting as more and more companies outsource their advertising and marketing budgets to freelancers to create e-mail marketing, print advertising, and website copy.

You may discover that your expertise lies in reading and reviewing others' work. Editing and proofreading fall into this category and are in high demand. Other authors will hire you to Beta-read, proofread, copy or line edit their fiction or non-fiction works.

Everyone has a story and many people want to share it. Just because we all have our own story does not mean that we were all meant to write it. Have you ever read someone's testimony and thought to yourself, "why in the world did he or she write it? Or, why didn't they have someone else write it for them?" These are the perfect candidates to hire a ghostwriter to document their story, autobiography or testimony. Whether it is of a traumatic event, a sordid past, or an inspirational journey, people want to get the information out for someone to read and be impacted by. A ghostwriter's responsibility is to take the original material in any format, written or verbal, and transform it into the written word in such a way that readers will enjoy and find appealing.

Ghostwriting is an ideal opportunity for someone who is looking to earn a living writing, but who may not necessarily be interested in the fame, recognition or acknowledgment. Unless otherwise specified by the client, a ghostwriter will not be listed as the author or even contributor of a work. If you are okay with that, ghostwriting may be a good online business for you.

A benefit of ghostwriting and the writing and editing world in general is that everything can be handled through the computer. A client can find you, discuss the job requirements and hire you without ever actually speaking with you. They can provide you with the specifications and you can ask questions along the way through e-mail and messages. Even the final product can be delivered and revised without any verbal communication if you choose to do so. Payment can be made by any number of means such as PayPal, CashApp, Venmo, Zelle or any other online financial institutions. Be sure though to guarantee that you are being paid by establishing some type of guidelines, schedule or milestones based on the nature of the project.

Here are just a few types of writing assignments that you may find interesting:

- Sales letters/e-mails
- Manuals
- Academic papers
- Business-to business correspondence
- Resumes and cover letters
- Christian books and testimonies
- Auto-biographies
- Webcopy
- Non-fiction how to or self-help books
- Fiction
- Poetry
- Short stories
- Case studies

The list goes on and the opportunities are limitless. As the world becomes more and more digital, the need for people to write copy to put out there will only increase, helping to sustain your business. Not every writing job pays the same amount of money, nor does it warrant a huge payout due to its size. Diversify your product offerings to help develop your business into a sustainable and long-term venture. You may decide that you do not like or have the creativity to write fiction stories, yet you can write amazing advertising and promotions or copyrighting which is a very profitable niche. Even if you are unfamiliar with the product or service being offered, with a little bit of research and some writing skill, you can certainly add this type of writing to your portfolio.

Writing may not sound like a sustainable business opportunity since in reality the quantity may be dependent upon how much material you are capable of producing. However, what if you were to work with a team of writers, each specializing in a different market, target audience or writing style, meeting a variety of customer needs. Now we are talking about not only a profitable business model, but one which can withstand the test of time, market changes, genre and even cross ages and industries.

Some facts about ghostwriting:

TOOLS:

SCRIVENER (For writers)

GRAMMARLY (Simplifies writing)

BIBISCO

MANUSKRIPT

SCRIBUS

- **Required skills**: ability to write, read and have a good grasp of the language (i.e. grammar and spelling). Have a desire to continuously learn and polish your craft. You will only get better the more that you write, edit and read.

- **Training and Learning Curve**: Medium. Some people may have the ability to jump right in and write something off the cuff. Others may require prompting, an outline or direction. Whatever style works best for you, you must still continue to learn. Consume all of the material that you can about the process through online courses, articles and books. There are also organizations which provide classes and membership opportunities so that you can communicate with other writers and authors and stay on top of best practices and new opportunities in the marketplace. American Writers and Artists Inc. (AWAI) is one such organization that even offers a monthly newsletter to keep you informed about trends and how to increase your earning potential.

- o   http://www.thebarefootwriter.com/
- o   https://blog.reedsy.com/freelancer/how-to-become-a-ghostwriter/

- **Passiveness Index**: Low. Since you will not be receiving any acknowledgment from you work, there is no possibility for residual or passive income to come rolling in. Once you complete the job or task, your earning potential for it ends.

- **Investment**: Little to no investment required. Although there is no initial outlay to begin writing, you should invest in classes, subscriptions and courses to improve your skills, understand the market and hone into those areas where you can best apply your expertise.

- **Reasonable monthly goal in one year**: Depending upon the type of writing that you are doing and how much time an effort you are willing to dedicate to the process, you can successfully earn $1000 - $5000 per month.

- **Risks**: Unfortunately, just because you are working from home and may have never met your client, they do not believe in the value of the service that you provide. They are not willing to pay your rate and want you to complete the same job for much less. Be careful of falling into this trap and writing your life away for little to no money. Your time is valuable. Find those clients who appreciate your skills and expertise and who are willing to pay for it.

  Writing can also be a very lonely profession. Sitting at your computer for hours on end, staring at the black and white of it all can be isolating, stressful and possibly bad for your health. Take this into consideration when you are considering your online business. Ask yourself if you can handle not having personal contact with your clients or others.

Another benefit of developing an online business by ghostwriting is the ability to work when you want, where you want, from the convenience of your home or lounging on the beach. There are many job sites out there to help you get your clients, including:

- <u>UPWORK</u>

All The links and tools listed in this book are available for free at www.emcpress.com in an easily clickable PDF File

- <u>FIVERR</u>
- <u>FREELANCER</u>
- <u>FLEXJOBS</u>
- <u>FREELANCE WRITING GIGS</u>

All The links and tools listed in this book are available for free at www.emcpress.com in an easily clickable PDF File

E-bay and Ecommerce selling platforms

With more than 152 million active users[xx] on eBay alone, selling goods online has become quite a lucrative business. If you have never visited the site, you are certainly missing out on the gold mine that can be found within eBay. From a buyer's perspective, you can find literally anything and everything that you want on eBay. Like Amazon, it is a depot or central location for customers to find and buy online and have their purchases shipped directly to them. There are several differences between the two:

- eBay transactions are typically completed as an auction; Amazon sales are retail.

- eBay vendors all own their own inventory and ship directly; Amazon owns most of the inventory and is responsible for shipping.

- eBay goods may be new or used while Amazon goods are generally brand new.

eBay caters to bargain shoppers who have scoured the Internet for the best deals. Like with any other online business, you are more likely to succeed if you are selling something that someone wants to buy. Whether it is new or old, be sure to do your research to identify those things that consumers will be searching for. Follow the trends, and even start buying small things. This will build your reputation on eBay since a lot of weight is placed on reviews of both vendors *and* buyers.

Selling on eBay may be a great way to begin your online store for those items that you are most passionate about. Remember when you looked at your skills and characteristics and the things that stood out to you as hobbies or interests. Maybe you collect figurines. You could certainly build a profitable business from the buying and selling of items like this, of course, if you properly price and market the items. Be sure to price your wares with enough margin to not only cover the cost of the item but all of your selling, payment and shipping fees where applicable. What about those antique clocks that you have been collecting for years and years!! Checkout the market and what other investors and collectors may be looking for. Using eBay to sell your products, you are not limited to only those enthusiasts within your social network or your niche club. Instead, you now can expose your items to a much larger audience, many of whom may be willing to pay above market value if they believe it has value, if it creates an emotional response in them.

This emotional response is critical to not only selling on eBay. Keep it in mind no matter what online business venture you go into. Think about the last time you decided to clean out your garage and hold a yard sale. Inevitably, someone will come along and discover amongst what you consider to be rubbish and junk, a gem or treasure that they have been searching for. As the saying goes, "one man's junk is another man's treasure". Just because you may no longer have a need for an item or find it to be junk, someone out there in the land of the world wide web will have a need or desire for it.

Besides eBay and Amazon, and although these are two of the most popular, there are several alternatives that you may also want to try selling your goods on.

- Rakuten (formerly known as Ebates) – most similar to Amazon

- Etsy – most similar to eBay in that it charges a listing fee. However, it is more focused on craft or hand-made items as well as vintage

- Craigslist – online Classified ads

- Newegg – best suited for tech products

- Shopify – a complete ecommerce store

- WooCommerce – a WordPress plugin which allows you to add ecommerce features to your own website.

The first items in this list are established sites where many vendors sell or auction off their products. The last two are slightly different yet still viable online business options. Shopify and WooCommerce are platforms where you as the business owner create your OWN online store rather than simply selling on someone else's platform. We will go a bit more in depth into how each of these can still help you build your online business in the next section about dropshipping.

Each of the online selling options as mentioned has its advantages and disadvantages and you should research each very carefully to ensure the proper match for your specific products. To develop a sustainable business that will provide you and your family with a nice income and lifestyle, consider diversifying the products and utilizing each of the sites as it is intended with your various products.

Let's look at how selling on eBay and other platforms stands up against our key indicators.

TOOLS:

CRAZYLISTER (E-bay Lister)

XSELLCO (Automated feedback software)

TERAPEAK (What to sell?)

STREETPRICER (Repricing Tool)

- **Required skills**. Good communication skills. Think like an entrepreneur. Good eye for "things" to identify niche, saleable items and if there will be demand.

- **Training and Learning curve**: Low. Compared to some other online businesses, there is a relatively low learning curve involved. By doing some basic research and utilizing the skills and resources that you currently possess, it is possible to quickly and easily create an online business. There are many articles, videos and blog posts available online to help you get started with your business venture including:

    o https://premeditatedleftovers.com/naturally-frugal-living/how-to-start-selling-on-ebay/

    o https://community.ebay.com/

- https://www.wikihow.com/Sell-on-eBay
- https://www.shopify.com/blog
- https://woocommerce.com/blog/
- https://www.lifewire.com/how-to-buy-and-sell-safely-on-craigslist-2487155

- **Passiveness Index**: Low. Selling on eBay or any of the other platforms will require daily contact, constant searching for items and products and continuous management of pictures, descriptions, inventory and shipping.

- **Investment**: Little to none. eBay does not charge any fees for your account so there is no outlay until the product sells. Then you will be required to pay selling fees for each item. However, if you build your pricing model strategically and carefully, you should be able to earn a profit even after paying your selling fees. Unless you plan on only selling items around your house, you will have to make an investment to purchase items to sell. Shopify and WooCommerce both charge monthly fees and will vary depending on the packages that you select.

- **Reasonable monthly goal in one year**: $1000 - $5000 depending upon what niche market you are selling in to and whether you sell as auction or retail.

- **Risks**: Because buyers cannot inspect items at all when buying from eBay, you as the seller are at the mercy of sometimes unsatisfied customers. By using excellent pictures, providing accurate descriptions and being forthright yourself, you have a better chance of avoiding any type of false claims or unhappy customers. You also may risk purchasing and reselling counterfeit goods unknowingly and could get caught up in some illegal activity unwittingly. Be careful to work with other reputable vendors. Lastly, as with all online businesses, there is always the risk of online scams, theft and fraud. Your online account or accounts are always at risk of being hacked, leaving you holding the bag and the responsibility for payments, charges and even your reputation.

The bottom line of online selling is that you can in fact create and operate a successful online business. It will require hard work, effort, everyday commitment and strategic sourcing to keep your expenses low. Profit margins are typically low in this arena and you have to take into account the associated costs of each platform that you use, marketing and advertising expenses and of course, shipping. Let's look at this last item in more detail as we talk about dropshipping.

Dropshipping

Dropshipping, in its most basic form, is a supply chain model in which you as the business owner do not actually maintain any inventory. It is the process by which you sell product and then transfer the responsibility of picking, packing and shipping to the manufacturer. Sounds like a win-win situation. You are acting as a middle man between the manufacturer or distributor and the end customer, promoting the product and facilitating the sale. This gives the manufacturer the ability to expand their reach, possibly targeting a new or different audience, generating news sales while not having to manage the marketing and customer retention side of the business. They can focus on product design, manufacturing efficiencies and shipping methods.

Statistics show that dropshipping is the route that the majority of online retailers are choosing with profits showing to be 18% higher than those following traditional stocking and shipping models. The benefits far outweigh the expenses and with so many products available, the possibilities are endless.

Of course, like with each of the previous online businesses we have discussed, the first step in the process is to determine the niche market that you will be focusing on, and finding the right products. Throughout this book, we have identified various methods of identifying products and/or services and niche markets. These same systems will be effective whether you are considering building your business via Amazon FBA, as a self-published author, as an affiliate marketer or of course, selling products on a platform.

As a refresher, you want to find products that have few competitors, have an existing demand, of course, are legal, and most importantly, meet customers' needs or solve a problem. If you simply jump in and begin your ecommerce business without taking these things into consideration, you will be setting yourself up for certain failure. Do your research and find the product or products that customers want, that create that emotional response we have been talking about, and will be profitable.

To ensure this last piece, profitability, which is certainly the reason that you are considering this venture at all, you must not only evaluate the market and audience, but the cost side as well. When selecting your product, you also have to consider where you are going to source the product from. Will the vendor be local or overseas? Will they offer you a wholesale rate? What will shipping costs be and how much margin can you include that will still make your pricing competitive? When considering your retail pricing for your online store, be sure to include seller's fees, shipping and taxes. Don't forget the taxes! No matter the business, this is one thing that you do not want to mess with…avoid having any trouble with the tax man!!

Although you believe you may have found the perfect niche market, you are passionate about the products and you can relate to the target audience, if sales of the product will not be profitable, you will need to walk away. Be prepared for this upfront. Keep it in the back of your mind that not every product or niche will give you the long-term, sustainable business that you are looking for. Do not get so caught up or chained to a product line that you lose sight of your mission. Markets change, vendors change products or go out of business and new ones enter. Your business success will be tied directly to your ability to stay on top of the trends, to roll with the fluctuation in the market and continually remain in contact with your customer base and audience.

Some tips for finding a profitable niche market for your dropshipping business:

- Small and lightweight. Smaller items of course have lower shipping costs and consumers have a higher likelihood of buying them online. Customers buying refrigerators and furniture may browse products online but may prefer to go to a brick-and-mortar store to physically pick up their item or have it delivered. Shipping for larger items will also eat into your profit margins.

- Non-seasonal. Don't limit your product offerings to those specific to a certain holiday or time or year. If you are going to offer these items, be sure your product offerings span many seasons, holidays and times of year. For example, if you are selling party supplies, you are more likely to attract customers at every time of year for holiday, party and celebration supplies.

- Avoid major brands. Major brands like Samsung or Apple have already saturated the market with competition and their own branding.

- Retail price. As with size, price will also be a factor in your niche market. Consumers are more likely to purchase items between $15 and $200 online than in the store. There is something about face to face with a salesperson or representative in store that still draws people to the traditional store. The value or worth that is placed on the item may prevent people from simply ordering online.

Now that you have identified your products and niche market, you have to find a supplier to maintain inventory and ship your products on your behalf. Consider your supplier as a very important business partner. Think about it! Without the physical product being shipped, you don't really have a legitimate business anyway. The supplier will have responsibility for creating a quality product, maintaining inventory, and shipping product to customers on time. Because they have such a huge role in your business, you want to choose wisely when selecting your supplier. Some things to look for in a dropshipper supplier:

- Reputation. Avoid working with a company who is brand new like you. Review the company's reputation and history as a supplier.

- Quality products. Make sure you check that the quality of the products is up to what you and your customers expect. Remember that if poorly constructed products are shipped out and customers are unhappy, it is *your* reputation at stake.

- Shipping. In our microwave society, most customers want products immediately, or rather as quickly as possible. If you are utilizing a supplier in China for example, ensure that they can offer a quick turnaround time from order receipt to shipping, with fast shipping at a relatively low cost.

- Cost. Of course, you are in the business to earn a profit. If your cost to purchase the product is high, you may price yourself right out of the market if the perceived value of the product is not there. In other words, negotiate your costs to be as low as possible so that once you add in all of the other fees, you can still earn a profit of 40% or more.

So, how do you go about finding a reputable supplier of your products? Similar to the process we discussed in Amazon FBA, there are companies like Alibaba that can provide you with lists and resources to find and communicate with suppliers in China. You may also do a Google search for "suppliers" or use Saleshoo.com which has more than 8,000 suppliers who have been verified.[xxi]

Oberlo, an online hub for dropshippers, has made the process even simpler for you. You can find products on their website and add them to your store. Since they have already established relationships with suppliers, all you have to do is market and sell. Once your customer places an order, it gets sent over to the supplier and shipped! You can focus on building your brand and expanding your reach.

Now that you have your target audience, your products and your supplier lined up, let's talk about some platforms where you can sell these products.

Shopify is an easy to use online platform that provides you with all of the tools and resources to develop your own online store, with customers navigating to your website to purchase goods and products rather than through a more generic selling site like eBay or Amazon. One of the draws for a business owner to join the Shopify community is the low requirement to be technically savvy. In other words, the platform has been designed for even the most novice of online business owners to successfully and quickly create and operate your store online.

Alternatively, WooCommerce allows you to add a plugin to your existing website if you have one to allow you to market and sell product easily. It is not only flexible but also affordable enough for the entrepreneur just starting out to get their feet wet in the ecommerce arena with the ability to expand as your business grows.

Dropshipping is a highly profitable business if you use good business sense and are diligent. By establishing good relationships with suppliers and building a solid reputation and brand, you can be very successful in developing not only a profitable business but one that will carry your family into the future. As markets change, new products emerge and others fade away, you can sustain the business for the long-term by continuously researching trends, likes and dislikes and continuing to nurture and develop your supplier relationships.

TOOLS:

ALIEXPRESS (Chinese suppliers)

CHINABRANDS (Chinese suppliers)

CLICKMAGICK

DROPIFIED

OBERLO (for Shopify)

SHOPIFY

ALIDROPSHIP (Wordpress Plugin)

WORDPRESS

DROPSHIP SPY

INVENTORY SOURCE

DOBA

- Required skills. Good communication skills. Think like an entrepreneur. Good eye for "things" to identify niche, saleable items and if there will be demand. Supplier negotiations.

- Training and Learning curve: Medium. Dropshipping is all the rave right now so with its popularity, there are many online courses targeted to the many platforms and avenues.
    - https://top10onlinecourses.com/best-dropshipping-online-courses/
    - https://www.salehoo.com/blog/what-i-wish-i-knew-when-i-started-dropshipping-
    - with-shopify

- https://www.shopify.in/guides/dropshipping
- https://www.oberlo.com/features

- Passiveness Index: High. Once you establish your ecommerce store, suppliers and have laid the groundwork to reach customers, you can certainly expect to have passive income rolling in. However, it will still require constant attention, research and marketing to expand your audience and increase your product line.

- Investment: Little to none. Shopify and WooCommerce both charge monthly fees and will vary depending on the packages that you select. Since you do not have to purchase and store inventory, your overhead and expenses are also very minimal.

- Reasonable monthly goal in one year: $1000 - $10,000 per month depending upon what niche market you are selling in to and the amount of time and energy you dedicate to the process.

- Risks: Low. There are some risks of product obsolescence, manufacturing or inventory delays, and shipping errors; all things which are out of your control. However, if you diversify your products and work with a variety of suppliers, you can minimize your risk

Turnkey Websites

Maybe in the evaluation of your skills, you have determined that you have excellent computer skills and a knack for design. Building and in fact, flipping websites is probably one of the most profitable online businesses that you will ever find. Not only can it be profitable, but it can provide you with a very nice passive income for years to come.

A turnkey website is in theory a website that is fully functioning, built on a legitimate business model, with high traffic and proven success. You can get in the market by using some of the skills, tools and resources that have been laid out for you in this book as well as your own to create websites and then flip them to earn a profit. You can help others who want to get into an online business yet may not have the skills themselves to create the business from scratch. In this case, it is a win-win for everyone involved.

Of course, the first step in building a website to flip is to identify the niche market which would be most profitable in the long run. In other words, who would be most likely to benefit from and be willing to pay for a well-established, profitable, pre-made website. Be sure to consider the key factors we have discussed previously which will determine success such as low competition and uniqueness. Once you have identified the niche, you need to develop a catchy and keyword optimized domain name. This is what is going to grab the attention of not only a prospective buyer but also the target audience.

Now, you can certainly earn a profit by selling the domain name at this point, especially if it is something that may be in high demand. However, you can earn an even greater profit if the domain is turned into an actual business, a turnkey business to be exact. There are various types of websites that would produce optimal revenue from its sale:

- Ecommerce sites. Of course, if a website is already profitable and earning consistently for you, it will have more value to a potential buyer who does not have to invest in startup, go through the learning curve or experience the risks associated with a new online business. As the definition of turnkey states, this would be a complete product for immediate use.

- Content sites. Websites that are monetized through affiliate marketing and ad placement.

- Software as a Service. Although SaaS as it is referred has not been discussed in this book yet, the term is used for any service-related product that is typically sold through a subscription basis.

Just as in the brick and mortar world of selling off businesses or franchises, when you sell a legitimate business, and based on the terms of sale, you may generate a consistent, passive income for yourself and future generations. There are even websites geared towards connecting sellers and potential buyers of turnkey websites, domains and apps such as www.flippa.com.

Flippa offers valuations of businesses, brokerage assistance and even legal advice in how to proceed with contract negotiations for the sale.

Another option in this business arena is to purchase underperforming websites or domains, make some necessary improvements or enhancements, and flip them for a profit. Like the concept of real estate flipping, it may require some investment of time and capital to bring the site to a stage where it is valuable and worth a higher price. However, with some research, and careful planning, this may be another avenue to generate both current and passive income.

Let's look at some indicators about turnkey websites and flipping:

TOOLS:

FLIPPA

WHOIS

AFTERNIC

FREEMARKET

- **Required skills**. Good communication skills. Think like an entrepreneur. Knowledge of domains, websites and applications.

- **Training and Learning curve:** Medium. Once you have an understanding and knowledge of building a website, you can replicate the process over and over again, building additional sites and selling them off as necessary. Since this is a very popular and up and coming online business, there are also many entrepreneurs offering online courses, blogs and articles to teach you how to do it as well.

    o https://turnkeynation.com/blog/

- https://yaro.blog/275/how-to-buy-a-website-and-flip-it-for-profit/
- https://www.udemy.com/website-flipping-for-cash/
- https://www.humanproofdesigns.com/how-to-flip-websites/

- **Passiveness Index**: Very High.

- **Investment**: Little to none.

- **Reasonable monthly goal in one year**: $10,000+ per month depending upon what niche market you are selling in to and the amount of time and energy you dedicate to the process.

- **Risks**: Low. Buyers may be skeptical if they are new to the market. Be sure to work with a company like Flippa to connect the right buyers and sellers. Of course, fraud is a huge risk for any online business and it is no different in the arena. Another risk is misjudging the market through your research and creating or buying a website that no one else wants to purchase. If you have created it yourself, you may be at risk of losing only your time and any small investment made to establish the domain and hosting. However, research carefully before making a purchase to understand its needs, its true value and if others may be in the market to purchase it as well.

Website flipping is certainly a viable, profitable online business that will prove to be sustainable for the long-term. Be smart, do your research and most of all, have fun with this online business.

Gaming

When we talk about gaming, we are not talking about betting and gambling as a business since we already discussed the legal aspects of it. Instead, let's focus this section on video games, entertainment, livestreaming and online subscriptions. With the massive trend in online gaming, there are also a variety of options for earning money from this expanding marketplace. There seems to be a videogame for everyone, from every walk of life; from shooting games to sports games, to building blocks and crafts, to educational games and even bulldozer games, gamers span every niche and interest that you can think of.

The gaming community spreads far and wide with gamers connecting with friends on all of their devices at every hour of the day. Although some may argue the validity or positive nature of video games, the reality is that the video game industry is massive and booming. More importantly, for you as an online entrepreneur, there is an opportunity for you to develop an online business around it. Using some of the techniques and tools that we have already talked about in this book and skills that you already possess, you can earn a nice living from online gaming and entertainment, selling subscriptions and SaaS, or Software as a Service.

As always, you must first do your research into the niche market and audience that you will target for your business. Through your self-evaluation, maybe you know that you are passionate about sports. There are currently video games for nearly every sport imaginable with new ones being launched regularly. The community of gamers is committed to perfecting their scores, achieving the highest results or beating the clock with forums, blogs and chats dedicated to the subjects. This is a perfect arena to learn the ins and outs of the gaming world, the mindset of a gamer and the needs and problems that exist that you may be able to solve.

By participating on the relevant social media platforms where gamers hangout, you can build your reputation as knowledgeable, experienced and trustworthy so that you can promote and sell your products and services. There are even several platforms that you can use to help you with your business:

- Twitch. Twitch is a popular site for streaming and viewing video game play.

- YouTube Gaming is similar to Twitch in that it is a highly utilized platform for the gaming community and discussions about gaming. The earning potential and path is similar in both as well.

- Mixer. Streaming for players from gaming systems like Xbox and PlayStation Live Platforms.

In developing your business plan in the gaming and entertainment industry, consider how you will utilize some, if not all, of the following techniques to earn revenue:

- Affiliate marketing
- Advertising
- Sponsorships. As an Influencer, you can earn money by endorsing products and services for other companies.
- Merchandise. Uniquely designed merchandise for your followers in the community.
- Subscriptions for viewing, gaming and access to features like emoticons, content and graphics.
- Online purchases, unlocking features and levels
- Videos or vlogs about gaming, techniques and tricks

A combination of each of these opportunities across multiple markets or platforms will open the door to a profitable and sustainable online business in gaming and entertainment.

Let's look at some of the indicators and requirements for a successful online business in gaming.

TOOLS:

TEMPLATEMONSTER (best templates for your gaming website)

Game Portal Website Template for Gaming Sites

OBS (Software for Game Streaming)

PATREON (Monetize your projects)

PLAYTEST

BETAFAMILY

BEST REVIEW APP

BETATESTING

CREATE YOUR OWN GAME

- Required skills. Passion for gaming. Video game knowledge.

- Training and Learning curve: Medium. If you are already a gamer, the majority of learning that will be required will be in the monetization as discussed in other areas of this book such as affiliate marketing, blogging, merchandise and videos.
    - https://www.lifewire.com/make-money-streaming-on-twitch-4144817
    - https://www.cnet.com/news/top-ten-gaming-blogs/
    - https://www.makeuseof.com/tag/6-ways-to-actually-make-money-playing-video-games/
    - https://mirillis.com/blog/en/how-can-you-earn-money-purely-from-gaming/
- Passiveness Index: High. Although it will not be a set it and forget it business and will require constant monitoring, it is possible to earn passive income through gaming.
- Investment: Little to none.
- Reasonable monthly goal in one year: $100 - $1000 per month depending upon what niche market you

are selling in to and the amount of time and energy you dedicate to the process.

- Risks: Low. Like anything on the Internet, the possibility of fraud is high and more importantly, hacking. There are more specific limits and rules for those under 18 and restrictions around child usage. Be sure to research any specific rules and regulations about your specific niche market as well as the legality of the type of gaming.

Affiliate Marketing

Affiliate Marketing is the process of promoting products or services for another company and earning a commission for each sale that is made directly from your referral. In the highly competitive world of the Internet, not having to market or sell your own product can be a tremendous advantage to you. With the virtual limitless number of items available, your options are also endless. In other words, by promoting items that are already available, you don't have to research and identify your own products to sell. You do however, still have to research and identify the niche market that you will target your marketing efforts to.

Whether you are looking to earn just a few extra dollars, or create a full-time online business, affiliate marketing affords you the luxury of working on your schedule, from the comfort of your home, or the beach (if that's your thing)! In fact, Affiliate Marketing could even be the perfect addition to your existing online business to earn some additional passive income.

Your earning potential with this online business is only limited by YOU and how much time and energy you are willing to put into it. There are plenty of Affiliate Marketers out there earning thousands of dollars per month. There are several key factors to driving traffic and ensuring success:

- Consistency. Be consistent with your messaging, your advertising and your time.

- Drive traffic. This is NOT a set it and forget it system. You need to be actively promoting and driving traffic.

- Plan. Like with any business or venture, you must have a plan or business strategy.

- Other people's products. Unfortunately, you have no control over businesses or products that you are referring people to. Changes in their products or strategies may be a limiting factor in your success.

- Start up requirements: None other than Internet access.

Let's look at how you would actually start an online affiliate marketing business. The first rule of thumb in affiliate marketing is that in order to be able to refer people to products or services, you must know something about it and be willing to endorse it. You would not encourage a friend or coworker to visit the website of a product or service that you know nothing about in real life, why would you do it in the virtual world! To get started, you may want to first focus on things that you are passionate about, have an interest in or are knowledgeable about as we have discovered in our initial evaluation. This will become your niche market. There are certainly areas in which there will usually be high demand since people are always looking for new information or to learn something including:

- Hobbies and crafts
- Health and Fitness
- Wealth
- Relationships

Within each of these areas, there are endless possibilities and you may even identify more with research.

As we talked about early in this book, to be successful as an entrepreneur, you need to focus on being a solution to someone's problem. Through affiliate marketing, you may in fact, refer someone to a product or service that just might change their life. This should be forefront in your mind as you evaluate your passions and interests as well as what subject areas are trending and people are searching for and reading. Since affiliate marketing essentially is an online referral system from which a marketer receives commissions when sales are generated from a referral, you want to be sure that you are referring customers to reputable, legal and legitimate businesses and products. This is where having knowledge of the specific niche market and your target audience comes in handy.

Let's look at an example. If you are a connoisseur of fine brandy, you don't want just any brandy. You have purchased, researched, and sampled many different flavors, brands and origins of brandy. Now, let's look at who would you target your knowledge and passion for brandy to. What type of person would visit your website or blog in search of information about brandy and then be interested in your recommendations? Of course, it would not be someone in search of a new fitness center or car dealership. Be the solution and provide the brandy enthusiast with the information that they are looking for.

After you have identified your niche market and your target audience, now you will need to tap into an Affiliate Program. There are literally thousands of opportunities out there for businesses that are offering affiliate programs, you just have to do your research. Here are just a few ideas to help you begin your search.

- eBay Partner Network. There are billions of product listings available to promote. Check out how this system works.

- Amazon Associates. Amazon Associates is a very reputable online business and offers a variety of opportunities to promote products.

- Clickbank. An online platform that sells digital products and services, with currently more than 200 million customers worldwide.

- High-ticket affiliate programs. Programs that offer higher than usual commissions for referrals and sales. Since this offers a great opportunity to earn higher profits, we will discuss it in more detail below.

No matter your niche market or target audience, you are certain to find an affiliate program to meet your needs. Just doing some simple Google searches and keyword searches will surely point you in the right direction.

If you are looking to build your affiliate marketing business into a long-term, profitable and sustainable business, you may want to consider high-ticket affiliate programs which offer higher commissions on referrals and sales. Although it sounds too good to be true, these types of programs will require you to target a higher level of client and the organization should provide you, the entrepreneur, with additional support for your efforts. For example,

- 1-on-1 coaching and step-by-step training on the product
- Funnel and sales pages with a proven conversion track record
- Rather than you being paid for only the first referral, affiliate programs for high-end tickets should provide you with the ability to earn for each subsequent purchase the customer makes.

Some niche markets which offer High-Ticket Affiliate programs include: debt relief services, health and wellness programs, gold and precious metal investments, legal injury, travel, and medical equipment. By doing some research, you can certainly find not only affiliate marketing programs in your niche but in some of these high-ticket niche markets as well.

Now that you have an affiliate program, you have to decide what social media platform you will utilize to reach the attention of your target audience.

There are various methods and platforms for marketing your newly aligned products and services and some platforms may be better suited over others. We have to first consider what your expectations are from social media related to your online business:

- What does your social media footprint currently look like?

- On which platform does your target audience primarily hang out on?

- What is the primary purpose for marketing on the Internet? Do you want to build brand awareness? Sell a product? Create a buzz? Add content to start a discussion?

By answering these questions, you will be able to determine which is the best platform to effectively and profitably market to your target audience.

Let's now look at each of these platforms and how it can best suit you to develop and operate your online affiliate marketing business.

Blog

According to a study by Statista.com, Tumblr alone had more than 463.5 million blogs as of April 2019.[xxii] Although this number is staggering and frankly, a bit scary and seems like a huge number of competitors, consider how many issues, topics, products and ideas are being discussed on these blogs. There are probably that many and more varying perspectives and thoughts being expressed. You can still make your blog stand out because of your own unique style, viewpoints, spin and preferences. A blog is a great way to share your personal perspective, build your audience and draw them in to your network.

Post material that will be appealing to your target audience. As we talked about earlier and in various sections, creating your online business is about providing the reader or potential client with what they want to read, what they are interested in and something that will solve a problem for them. It is not simply about driving traffic to your blog to pound your chest and say that you have a large following. The ideal topics and subjects that you write about will entice your audience because you have something to offer; a solution to their problem. In the end, your goal is to have them visit your blog and actually click, follow and purchase through the affiliate marketing links that you offer them.

If you are just starting out with a blog, select a domain name or name that will attract people to your site. For example, going back to my brandy example, www.thebrandyguy.com could be the domain name for my blog about all things brandy. As part of your plan to develop your business, you must decide how you are going to attract Internet surfers to visit your blog and view the products and services that you are promoting. In other words, decide what format you will express your thoughts and opinions to attract your intended audience to your blog. There are quite a few ways to do this. Let's look at a few:

- Review articles. A review article is your opportunity to share your opinions and preferences for a specific item or subject. For example, talk about your preference for a certain type of brandy with of course, the link for your follower to purchase it.

- How to Articles. You could write a How-To Article about something that you are very knowledgeable or passionate about. For example, let's say you have a lot of experience creating a blog or website. Create a how-to article to define exactly HOW to purchase a domain name and host provider and provide a link to the one that you use and promote.

- Product vs Product Articles. A Product versus Product Article is a comparison between two or more items or services, stating the pros and cons of each. Include the affiliate links for readers to follow and purchase one, if not all of your suggestions. For example, back to my brandy example again, your product vs product article could compare the benefits and qualities of one brand of brandy versus another. When the fellow brandy connoisseur follows the link you have provided, clicks on it and in fact, purchases the brandy, you will earn a commission.

- Listicles. Although you may have never heard of the word listicle before, I am sure you have seen these articles that appear in blogs in the form of a list. They range from short bullet points with a paragraph or two description to longer titles, summarizing a complete idea and usually containing a picture or catchy meme. There are various listicle options that authors use to attract and retain their reader's attention:

- Research based. These authors have done a tremendous amount of research in an area and want to summarize all of it in a more concise form. For example, "How to get Pregnant Fast". There are a lot of studies on this subject yet not every couple will take the time to research all of it. People want a quick reference guide to help them succeed at getting pregnant.

- Report based. Maybe you want to provide your audience a summary of what is going on with a particular situation or news event. Rather than providing all of the details, you write a short version or summary of how things are occurring or the future of something. For example, What's Next for the political party?

- Advice based. This type of listicle is usually based on some personal experience and research. It is not only informative but provides direction and guidance. For example, 7 Tips to Handle a

Bully or How I Cleared up my Acne in 7 days.

- o Easy Reference. This type of article will list out items that a reader can quickly read and use. For example, The 30 Best Places to Eat in Chicago or 25 Things to Use Q-tips for.

- o Personal or Editorial. In this type of listicle, the author is trying to get a certain point across or influence the reader. For example, 3 Reasons Why Men should receive Higher Pay than Women or 5 Important Things to Know about Investing in Small Stocks.

As in anything you are writing, listicles should have a purpose or value to your intended audience. Although they themselves will not generate any revenue, they are helping to attract an audience, to influence a reader, to generate buzz about you and even to promote products and services through your Affiliate Marketing links.

Moving on. When doing your research about hangouts, you may have realized that other types of social media are a better place for your content or promotions to reach your target audience. Let's look at some other online platforms which may be useful to you:

YouTube Channel

YouTube can be an effective and profitable way to reach your target audience since it seems to have something for everyone. No matter what you are looking for, someone has created a video about it. For example, what if you are at the lake and want to learn how to water ski. I am sure that there is a video out there to tell you how to stand up and maneuver on the water skis. Why not use it to visually tell your audience about your product review or How to do something! Be sure to provide the affiliate link to the product or service for the viewer to follow.

YouTube makes it super easy to upload your videos and no expensive equipment or video production is required. In other words, no huge outlay of money to get your video posted; you simply need your Smartphone and the willingness to record yourself talking about your topic.

We know that people spend a lot of time watching videos these days. As you create more and more videos, it is likely that you will create additional impressions or shares and viewers who watch, like and share your material. This truly is the beauty of all social media platforms.

Instagram/Instagram Ads

As a photo and video-sharing platform, Instagram inspires people to take action. By telling your story in a visual format, you can solicit that emotional response within your followers that we have been talking about, encouraging them to move forward with a purchase of a product or service. The point of Affiliate Marketing is to refer people to the goods and services that you are promoting with the expectation that they will purchase and therefore, you will earn a commission. Attractive and eye-catching pictures and videos are an excellent tool for you to draw attention to your products, your blog or website.

Facebook/Facebook Ads

According to a report about the number of Facebook users in 2018, there are more than 2.2 BILLION people around the world using Facebook.[xxiii] The Facebook platform offers an advertising system to allow you to reach a targeted and specific group of users. You want to ensure that target audience is seeing, liking, sharing and in fact, purchasing what you are promoting.

Solo Ads

A Solo Ad is an email broadcast to only those subscribers who have given their permission to be sent email offers. They are a great tool to drive traffic to your blog or website and create interest in your topic or discussion. Of course, your goal is for the reader to follow the link and to make a purchase.

Podcasting

Although podcasting is a highly competitive arena and social media platform, it does not mean that you should not be a part of it. A podcast is a series of audio or video files about a subject area or topic. Podcasts are usually scheduled episodes with each one leaving the audience anticipating the next one. Podcasts can help you to develop your brand surrounding your online business, build your reputation as an expert in the area, and very importantly, build a connection with your audience. We have talked throughout this book about reaching your target audience where they are at, or soliciting an emotional response from them. What better way to connect than for them to hear your voice or see you, to get to know your tone, your intent and your message.

Some people may not be comfortable being seen or heard by the public. They may be much more at home from behind the screen than in front of it. However, in today's digital world, people thrive on getting to know you and what you bring to the table. Using a podcast can differentiate you from the competition simply because a listener likes the sound of your voice or way you look.

Podcasting has become one of many digital formats of media that audiences can use to gain information. You see (or hear) people listening to podcasts during their daily commute in the car or train; in the office while they are working; late night when the house is quiet. In our busy society, listening to audio files has become for many the only way to read a book, learn some new information or catch up on the day's news. Why not take advantage of a captive audience and tap into this resource as well! It is also a great way to promote either your own or others' products and services through affiliate marketing links.

Of course, no matter which platform or combination you choose to use, be sure to create amazing content that your audience will find to be valuable in some way. Be the solution a problem!

Since your goal with your Affiliate Marketing Business is to earn a commission for each sale that is made directly from your referrals, you need to make sure that you have the right tools to help you maximize your impressions, your exposure and your conversions. Here are a few tools to help you get started with your affiliate marketing business:

- Auto-Responder. Draw attention to your products and services using automated emails to ensure more referrals and more commissions.

- Funnel Builder. A funnel is the process of guiding your target audience through the various stages from awareness to sales and there are many websites and tools to help you establish your funnel.

As an affiliate marketer, consider yourself as a brand ambassador. You are representing products and services on behalf of other entrepreneurs and companies and as they gain popularity, your reputation will increase as well. You can find affiliate marketing programs literally in EVERY market and niche and with dedication, hard work and diligence you are sure to grow your audience, expand your reach and ultimately entice your followers to purchase from those companies that you present.

Let's look at some of the indicators or requirements for developing a successful online business in affiliate marketing:

TOOLS:

CLICKMAGICK

VOLUUM

CLICKBANK

JVZOO

CJ

ADPLEXITY

AWIN

AFFISE

AFFLUENT

EVERFLOW

AFFTRACK

IMPACT

CLICKINC

TUNE

OPTIMIZEPRESS

LEADPAGES

AWEBER

GETRESPONSE

- **Required skills**. No special skills, qualifications or education. All you need is a computer and the desire to succeed!

- **Training and Learning curve**: Low. You will find a huge number of blogs, online courses and websites dedicated to affiliate marketing. Even Amazon has created videos to help you with their affiliate program.

    - https://affiliate-program.amazon.com/
    - https://nichehacks.com/profitable-niches-for-affiliate-marketing/
    - https://www.volusion.com/blog/top-5-benefits-of-affiliate-marketing/
    - https://www.shoutmeloud.com/how-to-make-money-with-amazon-affiliate-program.html

- https://makeawebsitehub.com/how-to-start-a-podcast/

- **Passiveness Index**: High. Once you have a foundation of followers and you have built a reputation of producing good content, people will continue to visit your site or blog for new and fresh information and will regularly follow your recommendations and suggestions for products and services. This will bring in passive income as they click and purchase on the same content or material you have already created.

- **Investment**: Little to none. There is no huge capital investment required to begin your Affiliate Marketing business and it is highly feasible to start your business with as little as a $100 investment in a blog or website.

- **Reasonable monthly goal in one year**: $5000 or more once you have selected a niche market and thoroughly capture the attention of your audience, building your reputation as trustworthy and knowledgeable.

- **Risks**: Low. Although there are some risks of joining an affiliate marketing program, they are relatively low. Promoting a less than reputable company or product could adversely affect your reputation. You can avoid this by carefully selecting those companies that you represent or promote.

As an example, let's look at how affiliate marketers were affected by MOBE. You may be familiar with this incredible online opportunity by MOBE, or My Online Business Empire, which was recently shut down by the FTC. It was an online training program that convinced a person to join for a nominal fee, only to then lure them to purchasing up to $20,000 in online training programs. Through its fraudulent marketing, MOBE led the victim to believe that he or she could learn to build a successful online business for just $49, but then sucked them into buying more and more services. When the business and website were shut down, the plug was also pulled on all of the affiliate marketers. Just an example of the risk you take when promoting a product or service.

Affiliate marketing is an excellent way to establish yourself and build an online business but in reality, it will not provide you with the sustainable long-term business that will support you and your family for the future. As products enter and exit the market, and businesses change, your opportunities will change as well. Although passive income is possible while you are actively promoting products and services, it will not go on forever without constant contact, massaging and care of your website, blog and affiliate relationships.

Online Courses

There has never been a better time to create an online business offering online courses than right now. According to the World Economic Forum, millions of people purchased courses online in 2017 to a tune of $255 billion. [xxiv] Creating and selling online courses, otherwise known as knowledge commerce, is certainly a viable online business which will provide you with a passive income for years to come.

In order to begin creating online courses as your business model, of course, the first step is to identify the niche or target audience to share your information and knowledge with. Online courses can range from how to create a blog to developing a five-star business and everything in between. As many areas of interest that you can come up with equals the number of ideas for courses and webinars.

As you are doing your research, remember to keep in mind several key factors as we have stressed previously: low competition, unique and/or an area possibly needing improvement. Let's talk about this last one for a minute. There may be an educational course that you took several years ago which you believe was good but things have changed and/or there may be some improvements that could be made to the subject matter. This may be an opportunity to reach the same market with an updated, fresh training course.

First, identify the audience who will be most interested in what you have to say. Then, focus on building your following through blog posts, online chats and communication. Build your reputation as knowledgeable and trustworthy all the while collecting information on what types of questions or issues your audience has. As discussed, you want to be the solution to a problem. What problem can you solve for someone by offering them an opportunity to learn through your course?

Online courses not only offer a solution to the viewer but will extend your reach as your participants share their knowledge with others, directing them back to you for future and additional course sales. The opportunity for passive income is very good as you can offer additional courses, including refreshers and new information.

In order to establish an entire online business using courses as the business model, you will need to diversify and offer classes in a variety of genre or topics. For example, you may want to focus in a broad subject area where you can offer a variety of classes, reaching multiple groups or types of audiences. Online courses can be used to attract potential clients to your coaching or other existing business, to build your brand recognition, or to share your knowledge.

Like with each of the online businesses we have discussed, it is important to identify a platform to use. Deciding on which is best for you will depend on your target audience, where they hang out, and what format do they prefer to learn in: video, interactive, webinar, self-taught.

- o Udemy – you must sell your course on their platform only at their recommended price. If you are just starting out in this market, this will certainly provide you with passive income.
- o Thinkific – all-in-one platform offering tools and resources to help you build your course, and market it to your target audience.
- o Kajabi – provider of online presence solutions
- o Teachable – allows you to sell your course on your own website or blog

Due to the low cost of development, creating an online course as a business or to add to your product offerings will certainly prove to be profitable and sustainable as online users remain hungry to devour all of the information they can.

Let's look at the indicators and factors for establishing online courses as a viable online business:

TOOLS:

OBS (Software for Screen Recording)

HITFILM EXPRESS (Video Editor)

DAVINCI RESOLVE (Video Editor)

VIMEO (Video Hosting)

OPTIMIZEPRESS (Landing Page Creator)

TALENTIMS (Course Creator)

PODIA (Course Creator)

- **Required skills.** Knowledge and expertise in a particular area. Computer skills. Learning Management System

- **Training and Learning curve:** Medium. Creating an online course is only one part of this business model. You must become an expert in the specific subject area and learn to present in such a way that solves a problem.

- https://www.thinkific.com/blog/online-course-business/
- https://blog.kajabi.com/kajabi-vs-teachable-which-online-course-platform-should-you-use
- https://www.thepennyhoarder.com/make-money/how-to-create-online-courses/
- https://socialtriggers.com/online-courses-create-and-sell/

- **Passiveness Index**: High. Once you have a foundation of followers and you have built a reputation of producing good content, people will continue to visit your site or blog for new and fresh information and will regularly follow your recommendations and suggestions for products and services. This will bring in passive income as they click and purchase on the same content or material you have already created.

- **Investment:** Low. Expenses will vary depending upon the path that you choose to develop your online course. Of course, your time is valuable as well and creating the course will require possibly 100 man-hours depending upon the topic.

- **Reasonable monthly goal in one year**: $5,000 - $20,000 per month.

- **Risks**: Medium. As with any online business, your business is susceptible to frauds, scams and customers who do not pay. However, in this arena, you also are faced with the risk of obsolescence, changes in the audience interests and in the subject matter. It is your responsibility as the business owner to continuously stay in tune with your community.

Additional Options for online businesses

As you can see, the possibilities for online businesses seems to be endless and we have only touched on a handful of options so far. In order to provide you with a full view and to get your brain working to possibly develop your own ideas and vision, let's look at some other amazing creative businesses that have been spawned from the Internet.

Airbnb is an online marketplace whose name is derived from "air mattress Bed and Breakfast". If you have never stayed at a B&B, you could either be in for a treat or a real surprise the next time you travel. A B&B is in reality a private home that its owners have decided to rent out bedrooms to travelers, usually providing breakfast with their stay.

This concept of Airbnb allows anyone to rent out their rooms as well through one central online directory, usually at prices less than a traditional hotel. Of course, there are some risks associated with listing your personal home, or a portion of it, for rent and usage by strangers such as damage to the property.

Airbnb may be a legitimate business with bookings and financial transactions being handled through a broker. Check out www.airbnb.com for additional information.

Stock Photos. Developers of websites, blogs, advertising, sales pages and books are all always in search of stock photos and images to use on their social media platforms. If you know your way around a camera, why not be the supplier of these images! You can even incorporate these into your own blog and articles to attract the attention of potential customers, talking about how you obtain your photos, where you get your inspiration and even your personal tips and tricks to taking great pictures.

Like any other online business, finding the right niche and target market for your photos is first and foremost. However, not only can this become a profitable business but you can earn passive income from your work, making it a sustainable long-term business. There is always something to photograph and someone willing to buy photos.

Branding. Custom branding has become very popular as more and more entrepreneurs are kickstarting their business ventures and are looking to get their products noticed. You can start your online business selling branded products that you design for your customers. Companies like Amazon, Lulu, Teespring and Zazzle, offer amazing support and guidance to help you get started on your journey of bringing custom merchandise to your fellow entrepreneurs and businesses. With no inventory to stock, no equipment to maintain, you can reap the benefits of the sale without the hassle of production. As more and more vendors enter the online marketplace, this business opportunity will continue to expand and grow. Why not get on board now and check out some of the resources at https://developer.amazon.com/merch.

Now, before you go on to the Conclusions, if you enjoy reading this book, please take thirty seconds to **leave me a review**. Find the direct link to the Amazon Review Page on the PDF you downloaded from **www.emcpress.com**. Thank you!

So, the entire password to get the PDF: letsstayintouch

The PDF summarizes the business assessments contained in this book, plus a list of extremely useful, online tools in a printable, **clickable**, handy, on-the-go version.

You will also find **ALL the links** listed in this book so that you can easily visit the resources suggested through the Chapters with your computer.

Please go to **www.emcpress.com** to get it NOW!

Just enter your email address, the password "letsstayintouch", and enjoy!

SUMMARY

By now, I hope it is clear that there are an infinite number of possibilities, target audiences, products and topics for you to research and develop into an online business. Having an entrepreneurial heart, and your unique qualities and skills, you are now ready to step into the digital world and reach your target audience.

No matter what your personal reason is or your 'why', the Internet opens a world of opportunities that most of us could never have imagined. It is my hope that through "Making Money from Home" I have been able to alleviate some of the fear and concern that you may have had towards starting an online business and provided you with a solution to *your* problem!

We have talked about the many common qualities of entrepreneurs in general including positivity, passion, curiosity, and independence. You will find that each of these characteristics will be beneficial in your pursuit of success, providing you with a foundation, drive and motivation to reach your goals.

We discussed the many benefits of becoming an entrepreneur including managing your own time, spending time with family and friends, being responsible for generating your own income and of course, pursuing your passions. We have walked through the process of identifying your skills, assessing your opportunities, becoming aware of the risks and selecting the right opportunity for you based on your own unique qualities and characteristics.

Let's summarize some of the many opportunities for you to make money from home by developing an online business:

- Amazon FBA
- Self-publishing on Amazon
- Ghostwriting
- eBay and Ecommerce platforms
- Dropshipping
- Turnkey websites
- Gaming
- Affiliate Marketing
- Online Courses
- Additional Options

Each of these opportunities brings with it its own advantages, benefits and risks. However, as you begin to research, plan and development your own personal online business, consider how you may be able to utilize some, if not all, of these options in combination to produce the most profitable, sustainable and long-term business model for your family and your future generations.

Of course, the digital world that we live in is a scary place but you have at your disposal a multitude of resources, support and help from many other entrepreneurs who have come before you, struggling, stressing and yet succeeding. Understand the skills that you already possess as well as the ones that you will have to expand.

Use this book as a resource and a guide as you move forward, referring back to it for support and information. Of course, as we have talked about, the digital world changes faster than the speed of light, and new opportunities and risks will surface each and every day. However, one thing is certain. As you learn, become more aware of the Internet's capabilities, and are connected with customers' needs, you too will have more opportunities and skills to present to the world, giving you a greater ability to be a solution to someone's problem.

I hope that I have demonstrated how the many benefits and advantages of becoming an online entrepreneur can not only impact your life, but in fact change the trajectory of it completely for you and your future generations. I understand you may still be experiencing fear and anxiety towards starting down this path. However, it is my sincere hope that I have inspired and motivated you to know that it is not only possible to start an online business, but that you can create a profitable, sustainable and long-term business. I hope that this book will be a catalyst for a new beginning.

Be true to yourself and enjoy the process!

If you enjoyed reading this book, please don't forget to **leave me a review** on Amazon as it is vital for my work and for other future entrepreneurs. Find the direct link to the Amazon Review Page on the PDF you downloaded from **www.emcpress.com**. You don't need to search for the product and waste your time, you'll find the direct link into the PDF and on the website. **Thirty seconds for you, worth a lot for me.**

Thank you,

Larry B. Fossett

All The links and tools listed in this book are available for free at www.emcpress.com in an easily clickable PDF File

---

[i] https://www.entrepreneur.com/article/197608
[ii] https://www.forbes.com/sites/andreamurphy/2018/09/20/the-2018-digital-100/#773a31316137
[iii] https://www.incomediary.com/top-young-entrepreneurs-making-money-online
[iv] https://wanderingaimfully.com/iwearyourshirt/
[v] https://www.merriam-webster.com/dictionary/
[vi] http://www.thelawofattraction.com/what-is-the-law-of-attraction/
[vii] https://www.quora.com/What-is-that-feeling-of-being-passionate-about-something
[viii] https://www.womenonbusiness.com/why-curiosity-is-the-most-important-trait-an-entrepreneur-can-have/
[ix] https://www.brainyquote.com/quotes/colin_powell_121363
[x] https://www.statista.com/topics/871/online-shopping/
[xi] https://www.merriam-webster.com/dictionary/business?utm_campaign=sd&utm_medium=serp&utm_source=jsonld
[xii] https://en.wikipedia.org/wiki/Multi-level_marketing
[xiii] https://www.investopedia.com/ask/answers/071614/whats-difference-between-binary-options-and-day-trading.asp
[xiv] https://www.forbes.com/sites/laurashin/2014/11/20/5-sophisticated-work-from-home-scams-and-how-to-spot-them/#47bc81d574e5
[xv] https://about.usps.com/future-postal-service/gcg-narrative.pdf
[xvi] https://www.reference.com/business-finance/unethical-business-practices-75f910133a4ced5
[xvii] https://en.wikipedia.org/wiki/History_of_the_Internet
[xviii] https://thewritelife.com/self-publishing-on-amazon-450000/
[xix] https://thewritelife.com/7-ways-to-make-money-writing/
[xx] https://www.thebalancesmb.com/make-a-living-selling-on-ebay-1794700
[xxi] https://www.salehoo.com/blog/how-to-start-a-drop-shipping-business-in-5-easy-steps

[xxii] https://www.statista.com/statistics/256235/total-cumulative-number-of-tumblr-blogs/
[xxiii] http://www.businessofapps.com/data/facebook-statistics/
[xxiv] https://www.thinkific.com/**blog/online-course-business/**

www.ingramcontent.com/pod-product-compliance
Lightning Source LLC
Chambersburg PA
CBHW021817170526
45157CB00007B/2617